I0021049

WordPress On-Site SEO 2021

Optimize Your WordPress Site for Better Rankings!

By Dr. Andy Williams

ezSEONews.com

Version 1.0
Updated: 19th February 2021

What People Have Said About Versions of This Book

The original version of this book was published in 2013. This edition brings the subject of WordPress On-Site SEO right up to date. The book has had major re-edits and all new sections. Some sections have even been removed altogether as no longer relevant.

The following comments are from customers over this timespan and may refer to any one of the major versions released.

"Very good book not only for WordPress SEO but any site SEO - explains the concepts behind tweaking your site I learned a lot from this book - it is now my guide to the world of SEO" **Gfergy**

"If you are using, or intend to use, WordPress as your website development platform, you NEED to read this book if you want to maximize your organic traffic.

I've been following Dr. Andy's work for the last decade or so and have always structured my websites along the principles he describes and I'm happy to report that they've sold a tad over £9M since 2003 (That's not the same as profit Mr. HMRC) based at least partly on organic traffic." **Pete Bennett**

"I am a huge fan of Dr. Andy's writing and have virtually all his books. The two reasons for this are a) he puts in the research time and has excellent analytical skills and b) he can put technical points across in a way that even a non-technical person such as me can understand.

This book is no exception to the rule. If you run a WordPress blog and you want to get visitors, this book is a no-brainer." **Pearson Brown**

"This book has plenty of screenshots showing very clearly what to do. It is not excessively technical like many internet books. This is important because every business person needs a website but most of us have neither time nor inclination to become IT experts, that time would be better spent on perfecting our own trade or profession." **Aquilonian**

"Just what a near-Luddite like me needs to hold my hand through refining my WordPress website. I definitely recommend this book for you non-techies out there." **Mike R**

Contents

DISCLAIMER AND TERMS OF USE AGREEMENT

How to Use This Book

This book will take you on a journey that is best followed in the order it is presented. At least for the first time. Once you have been through the entire book, it then works well as a "dip in when you need it" type reference book.

This book is not intended to teach you how to use WordPress, so you will need a reasonable working knowledge of WordPress. There are links to my books and courses at the end of this book if you need a refresher course on WordPress.

A Note About UK v US English

There are some differences between UK and US English. While I try to be consistent, some errors may slip into my writing because I spend a lot of time corresponding with people in both the UK and the US. The line can blur.

Examples of this include the spelling of words like optimise (UK) v optimize (US).

The difference I get the most complaints about is with collective nouns. Collective nouns refer to a group of individuals, e.g., Google. In the US, collective nouns are singular, so **Google IS** a company. However, in the UK, collective nouns are usually plural, so **Google ARE** a company. This is not to be confused with Google "the search engine" which is obviously singular in both.

There are other differences too. I hope that if I have been inconsistent anywhere in this book, it does not detract from the value you get from it.

WordPress itself will have some differences depending on whether you are using UK or US English. The one I find most obvious is in the labeling of the areas containing things you have deleted. E.g., comments or posts/pages.

If you installed WordPress with US English, you'll see this called "trash":

But if your WordPress is installed with UK English, this becomes "bin":

There are other places in the dashboard that use localized words like this. I'll leave those for you to find.

Found Typos in This Book?

Errors can get through proof-readers, so if you do find any typos or grammatical errors in this book, I'd be very grateful if you could let me know using this email address:

typos@ezseonews.com

Introduction

Search Engine Optimization (SEO) is the process webmasters go through to encourage search engines to rank their pages higher in the search results. Typically, it involves working on the site itself. This is called on-site SEO, but it also involves working at site promotion, and that is what's known as off-site SEO.

Sites can be built in a number of different ways (PHP, HTML, Flash, etc.), using a wide variety of site-building tools, with common examples being Dreamweaver, Drupal, and WordPress, to name just three. Most websites and blogs share certain features that we can control and use to help with the on-site SEO. These features include things like the page title, headlines, body text, ALT tags, and so on. In this respect, most sites can be treated in a similar manner when we consider on-site SEO. However, different platforms have their quirks, and WordPress is no exception. Out-of-the-box WordPress doesn't do itself any SEO favors, and can in fact, cause you ranking problems. This book will concentrate specifically on the on-page SEO of WordPress sites, highlighting the problems and working through the numerous fixes.

By the end of this book, your WordPress site should be well optimized without being over-optimized (which is itself a contributing factor in Google penalties).

NOTE: This book assumes you are familiar with WordPress. If you are a complete beginner, I would recommend you take the time to learn the basics of WordPress. At the very end of this book, you'll find links to my other books and video courses.

1. The Biggest Sin - Duplicate Content

One of the main considerations when working on a WordPress site is duplicate content. For example, every post you create will also be posted on several other web pages within the site. Whether that post is shown in its entirety on all these pages or as a shorter excerpt is often controlled by the site's theme. Some themes will let you choose, whereas others will not.

So, What Does This Mean to You, the SEO?

When a post is made on a WordPress site, it may be published in full on all of the following at the same time:

1. Homepage

2. Post page. Every post is given its own web page.

3. Category page(s). Posts are assigned categories, and the category pages show all posts in that particular category.

4. Date archive page(s). These are pages that show all the posts made on a given date.

5. Tag page(s). Tag pages are another way of organizing your content. You can assign several words or phrases to each post, and for every word or phrase, a tag page is created. These tag pages show all posts that have been tagged with a specific word. Therefore, if you used a tag blue widget on five posts, the blue widget tag page will show all five posts.

6. Author page. This is an archive showing all of the posts made by a particular author.

7. Multiple RSS feeds.

That's seven areas where the exact same post may show up!

If you assign just one category to a post and one tag phrase, that means each post could appear on seven areas of the site **AT THE SAME TIME**. While I recommend you only assign a single post to just one category, tags are different. If you use tags, I'd recommend 3-5 per post. That would take the count up to 10 – 12 pages showing identical content.

This type of duplication is bad.

So, the general rule that I recommend is to only include the full post on ONE web page of your site. On any other page where that post appears, you should be using excerpts, or in some cases, just the title.

Having a high level of control is vital to removing this type of duplication, and the process begins by choosing a good template. The template should allow you to specify what you want to be posted on each of those six areas of potential duplication. I will, therefore, look at themes shortly and explain what you need to look for when choosing a theme of your own.

First, though, we should mention web hosting.

2. WordPress Web Hosting

OK, so you may be wondering why I am talking about web hosts. After all, isn't this supposed to be a book about WordPress SEO?

Yes, it is. However, the speed at which your site loads (and even the uptime of your site) are factors that are taken into account by search engines. Slow-loading websites, or those which are unavailable for long periods (because the host server is down), suffer poorer rankings because of it. Sites that go down frequently, negatively impact the reputation you have with your visitors too.

There are many types of web hosts and lots of different plans that come with each one. You can get shared hosting, a managed or unmanaged Virtual Private Server (VPS), or a Dedicated Server. There are even some hosts that specialize in WordPress site hosting (although not all that advertise WordPress hosting are set up specifically for it). I also know of one host that specializes in hosting WordPress sites that are built with the Genesis WordPress theme.

So, which should you go for?

Well, that will depend on how much money you have available for your hosting. If you have a good budget, I would recommend going with a true WordPress optimized web host. WP Engine is one of the better known, though this type of hosting is not cheap, starting at $25 per month billed annually for just one site.

https://ezseonews.com/wpengine

A 10-site package would cost around $95 per month, also billed annually.

Do read the small print, though, if you decide to go with WP Engine. There are limits to the number of monthly visitors, local storage, and bandwidth.

If you are on a budget, then shared hosting may be a better option. I use shared hosting for a lot of my sites. You can see my currently recommended host and registrar here:

https://ezseonews.com/dwh

Your site won't be as fast as a premium host like WP Engine, but it is a trade-off between what you want to pay and the quality of the service.

2.1. CDN (Content Delivery Network)

Make sure your host supports a CDN, preferably free of charge.

CDN stands for Content Delivery Network. The name gives you a very good idea of what this does. It's a network of computers that deliver content. In this case, web pages.

Here is the definition of a CDN from Wikipedia:

Content delivery network <

A content delivery network, or content distribution network, is a geographically distributed network of proxy servers and their data centers. The goal is to provide high availability and performance by distributing the service spatially relative to end users. Wikipedia

That's a little technical. Here is another definition from Webopedia:

A Content Delivery Network (CDN) is a system of geographically distributed servers that work together to provide fast delivery of Internet content. It's designed to minimize latency in loading web pages by reducing the physical distance between the server and the user. A CDN allows for a quick transfer of assets needed to load content such as HTML pages, javascript files, stylesheets, images, and videos. A well-configured CDN can also help protect against common malicious attacks such as Distributed Denial of Service (DDoS) attacks. Over half of all internet traffic is served by CDNs.

Again, that's a little technical.

The bottom line is that if your website uses a CDN, then your web page will be served from several computers around the world. If someone in Australia tries to view your web page, then the CDN will serve up a copy of your page from Australia. If someone in Germany tries to view your web page, the CDN will serve a copy of your page from Germany. By matching visitor location to the CDN server, web page load speeds are minimized.

You should use a CDN if you have access to one. It had a dramatic effect on both load times and the reliability of my websites when I started using one. You'll see the actual server response time graphs from one of my sites in the next section.

A CDN does not have to cost you anything. Some web hosts include one with the hosting plan. The web host I use and recommend does.

2.2. Shared Hosting & Dedicated Servers

Most hosts offer a wide range of packages, from simple shared hosting to dedicated servers (where you are given a computer and told to get on with it).

Dedicated servers, and unmanaged VPS hosting, both require a certain level of technical know-how, so I don't recommend you consider those unless you are technically capable.

For most people, shared hosting will be the best option because of the lower costs, especially for new sites. However, shared hosting is generally the most unreliable in terms of uptime and server response times (how long the server takes to respond to a request to show your web page).

I recommend you test any host you are considering working with. If you know of a website that is hosted with a particular company, I suggest you sign up for a website monitoring service and keep an eye on the website uptime and server response times (essentially how quick and reliable the web host is). UpTimeRobot is a free service you can use, so search Google for that.

Monitoring a website on a particular web host will give you a good idea of how reliable that hosting company is.

3. Themes & Theme Settings

There are lots of great themes out there; many of them are free. I don't generally recommend free themes, and here's why:

- They may not get updated.

- Some might include malicious code.

- A number of them contain footer links back to the creator's website (or any website they choose), which is bad for SEO.

- They could be poorly written, and therefore slow to load.

Themes are very much a personal choice and depend on the type of site you are building. It is, therefore, difficult for me to recommend a theme to you. However, to get you started, check out these two that I often use myself:

1. Genesis Framework and associated child themes.
   Genesis is a framework that you install in your dashboard. It works as a "parent" theme, where its power comes from the dozens of child themes it can work with. Check out http://ezseonews.com/studiopress to see the full range of themes it offers.

2. Elementor Pro (if you want to design your own theme).
   Elementor Pro is my favorite theme. In fact, it isn't a theme, it's a plugin, but it allows you to create your own theme. As a design tool, it's flexible, stable, and allows you to design the website you truly want. Check it out at https://ezseonews.com/elementor

When you come to choose a theme, there is a checklist to take into consideration:

The theme MUST:

1. Load quickly.

2. Allow you to control how posts appear on all of the six potential duplication areas of your site that we looked at earlier. You should have the options of a full post, excerpt, or just the title.

3. Allow one (or two) menus at the top of the website.

4. Not include any mandatory links or attributions in the footer.

Points 2-4 can be answered by the theme's support desk. What about the first point, though? How can you tell the load speed of a website and check for potential problems with a template? You'll be pleased to know that this can be done quickly and simply.

For this, we can use a free service at GTMetrix.com

GTMetrix allows you to analyze the page load times of any web page you want.

Find a site that uses the theme you are interested in using, and enter the URL of that site into GTMetrix. This tool then breaks down the page load speed into elements and tells you exactly how long each element takes to load.

First, the summary:

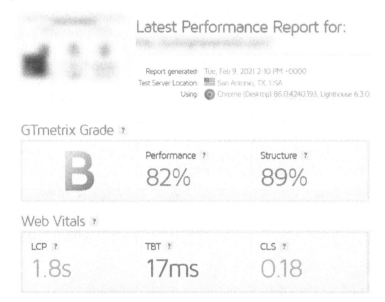

The summary gives you an A, B, C, D, or E rating for page speed. You also get to see the page load time in seconds, the total page size, and the number of requests that were needed to download the page, and lots of other useful information.

You should be trying to get an A or B for the GTMetrix Grade. Obviously, the lower the page load time, the better. I typically try for under 1.2 seconds for the LCP you see in that screenshot above. LCP stands for Largest Content Element.

Under the main summary are six tabs:

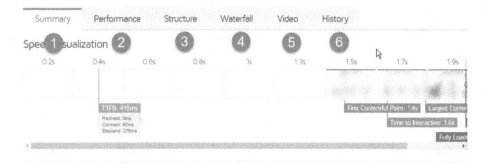

The summary shows a diagrammatic overview of how the web page loads, with the timings. To the right of this summary, you'll see some important times:

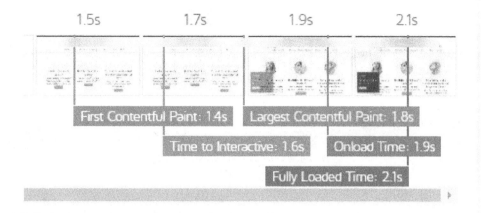

So this page has an LCP of 1.8 seconds, which is a little slow, and a full load time of 2.1 seconds. That's not bad, but it could be better.

Further down the page, you'll see the top issues affecting the page load time:

Top Issues

These audits are identified as the top issues impacting your performance.

IMPACT	AUDIT	
High	Eliminate render-blocking resources	⌄
Low	Avoid large layout shifts	⌄
Low	Use passive listeners to improve scrolling performance	⌄
Low	Use a Content Delivery Network (CDN)	⌄
Low	Serve static assets with an efficient cache policy	⌄

Each section can be expanded to get more information on the issue and how to fix it.

The Page Speed and YSlow tabs offer advice on how to speed up the website. Click on any entry in these tables for an expanded view that shows you specifically what you need to do to fix an issue.

You'll also find a graphic showing the size and page requests for elements on your page:

If you want more details on the exact timings of the page load, see the **Performance** tab.

The **Structure** tab will give you more details on issues and how to fix them.

My favorite tab for troubleshooting is the **Waterfall** tab. This one shows you a waterfall table of the elements as they load, including exact timings:

This is where you can get information on any theme-specific problems.

The URL column shows you the resource being loaded, and the Timeline column shows a bar with timings. Here is the timing data for the style sheet of this theme:

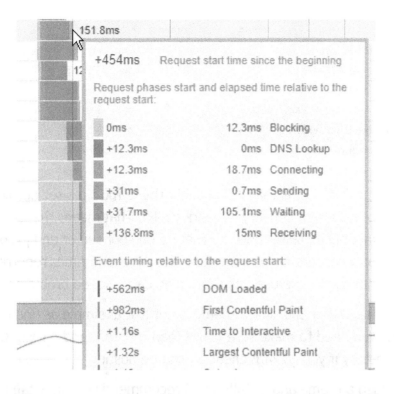

By looking for slow-loading elements on the page and checking whether they are related to the theme you want to use, you can make judgments on how well that theme is optimized.

TIP: You will find that a lot of the slower loading elements on a page are images. Some images are related to the theme, whereas others are not. Don't worry about slow-loading images that are not part of the theme.

Other issues can be linked to slow loading plugins and third-party widgets:

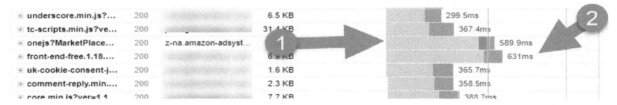

The first bar in that screenshot refers to an Amazon widget that takes 589.9ms to load. The second is a WordPress plugin taking 631ms to fully load. Obviously, these are not caused by the theme, so they should be ignored when evaluating a theme.

Also, look for any element that has a large file size as these take longer to download. There is a column that shows you the size of each element. Be careful, though, as some of these are in bytes (B) whereas others are in KB (Kilobytes, or 1000 bytes):

URL	Status	Domain	Size ▲
＋ fa-solid-900.woff2?...	200	.com	79.3 KB
＋ fa-brands-400.woff2...	200	.com	77.6 KB
＋ 2014-12-18_13-44-0...	200	.com	35.8 KB
＋ tc-scripts.min.js?ve...	200	.com	31.4 KB
＋ jquery.min.js?ver=3...	200	.com	31.3 KB
＋ tc_common.min.cs...	200	.com	28.7 KB
＋ aftersmall_thumb.j...	200	.com	20.8 KB

One final thing to be mindful of is that it's unlikely the demo sites set up by theme vendors use caching plugins or a content delivery network (CDN). That means the speeds you see with tools like this will probably be faster once it is set up on your server and properly optimized. With this in mind, don't concentrate too much on the page load times reported, and instead, look for large files that the theme uses, as these may cause speed problems on *any* server.

Hopefully, you have seen that choosing a theme is not just as simple as finding one that looks good and using it. You need to make sure it will load fast too, and not contribute to longer loading times, especially if you go with cheaper, shared hosting.

Once you have chosen a theme and installed it, I recommend you **uninstall** all other themes that may be in your WordPress Dashboard. The reason for this is that old themes can often be routes taken by hackers to gain access to your site. We don't want to give them that chance!

4. Google Tools

Google offers some great tools and advice to the webmaster for free. I use them, and I recommend you do too. The two recommended tools are:

- Google Search Console.

- Google Analytics.

I also recommend you read and learn Google's Webmaster Guidelines.

Links to all of these can be found on the resource page for this book here:

https://ezseonews.com/wpseo

4.1 Google Search Console

Why should you use Google Search Console (GSC)?

Here are some good reasons:

- Get notified by Google if there is a problem with your site. Google will send you messages if, for example, your backlink profile looks spammy, or if your site is using an old version of WordPress, etc. It will also notify you if it detects malware on your website.

- Discover any HTML problems with your site. You can then follow the suggestions that GSC gives you to resolve the issue(s).

- Submit and check your sitemap (which can speed up the indexing of your website).

- Select a geographic target audience. For example, if your website targets UK customers, but your site uses a .com extension, you can use GSC to tell Google that you want your site to be given more consideration in the UK.

- Check how well your site is being indexed by Google.

- Identify crawl errors. Google will tell you the URLs that it had trouble crawling and the page that linked to that URL, thus allowing you to quickly identify and fix broken links on your site.

- Request Google removes specific URLs from their search results.

- Get a complete list of all links that point to your website (at least the ones that Google knows about). This can be very useful, especially in identifying links from spammy sites, which you can then disavow with the Google Disavow tool.

- Identify keywords that people are using to find your site. Google shows you the number of impressions in the search engines, how many clicks you got, the click-through rate (CTR), and the average position in the SERPs (Search Engine Results Pages). The CTR can be very useful for finding pages that may need their title/description tweaked to try and improve the CTR.

GSC offers a useful set of tools for all webmasters. I highly recommend you sign up and add your website(s) to your account, so you can track them all.

4.2 Google Analytics

Google Analytics is a free visitor tracking tool, which is far more powerful than many available commercial tools.

Reasons to use Google Analytics (GA) include:

- See details of your visitors, like the search term they used to find your site, how long they spent on your site, which browser they use, what country they come from, and so on.

- Get real-time statistics showing how many people are on your site right now, and which pages they are viewing, etc.

- Connect your Google Analytics account to your GSC account, and Google AdSense account for even more tracking features.

- Split-test different versions of, for example, a sales page.

- Set up custom alerts to notify you about the things that are important to your business.

- Monitor mobile traffic.

- Lots of other features...

Once you have signed up for Google Analytics and registered your site with them, you'll be given some tracking code to insert into your web pages. Some themes will have an easy way to add your Google Analytics code, while others won't.

If you cannot find an easy way to add the tracking code, I would recommend you look for a WordPress plugin called "Header and Footer." This plugin will let you insert the code into the header or footer of every page on your site. I like this particular plugin because it has a lot of other features I regularly find useful (like inserting code before, after, or within a post/page's content).

4.3 Google's Webmaster Guidelines

Google's Webmaster Guidelines is a collection of articles detailing what Google likes and dislikes. If you own a website, you should be reading these guidelines and taking notes.

You can find a link to the guidelines here:

https://ezseonews.com/wpseo

The Webmaster Guidelines are divided into several sections:

- General Guidelines - advice on how you can make sure Google finds and understands your pages.

- Quality Guidelines – SEO advice, including what not to do. A lot of the WordPress SEO advice I'll give you in this book relates directly to these guidelines. They are VERY important.

5. WordPress Settings Menu

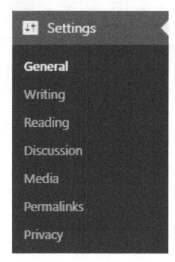

During the initial setup of a WordPress site, it's a good idea to go through the Settings menu first to make sure everything is set up properly. You will find this settings menu in the left sidebar of your Dashboard. Mouse-over the word **Settings,** and a popup menu will appear displaying the options. Click on the word **Settings,** and that menu integrates into the sidebar below the main Settings heading.

Let's go through the settings that are relevant to SEO.

5.1. General Settings

Site Title & Tagline

The top two items in the General settings are Site Title and Tagline. The Site Title and Tagline entered here will be displayed at the top of every page on your site. You can replace this with a logo image if you want, but how to do that will depend on the theme you are using. Each theme will have slightly different instructions for adding a logo, and logo dimensions will also be theme-specific.

Don't be tempted to stuff keywords into the site name or tagline fields. Your site name will most probably be based on your domain name, and the tagline should be a short sentence specifying your site's goal, philosophy, or slogan.

There is a good article on creating a tagline on the Copyblogger website called "How to Create a Rock-Solid Tagline That Truly Works." Read it here:

http://www.copyblogger.com/create-a-tagline/

If you need help with yours, I suggest you read that.

E-mail Address

The only other setting we need to concern ourselves with on this page is the email address. This will be used by WordPress, plugins, and a free external service (Gravatar.com). We'll be looking at these later, so your email address needs to be correct.

5.2. Writing Settings

In terms of SEO, the only setting we need to look at is the **Update Services**. These are a list of web services that get notified whenever new content gets published on your site.

Update Services

When you publish a new post, WordPress automatically notifies the following site update services. For more about this, see Update Services on the Codex. Separate multiple service URLs with line breaks.

```
http://rpc.pingomatic.com/
```

If you see this:

Update Services

WordPress is not notifying any Update Services because of your site's visibility settings.

..then you have checked the **"Search Engine Visibility"** box in the Reading settings. We'll cover that in a moment.

Basically, every time you post new content (or edit old content) on your site, a message is sent to all "services" in this list (currently just Pingomatic) to let them know there is new content. They will then come over to your site to see what new content you have published.

This list helps your content get noticed and included more quickly in the search engines. WordPress installs just one service, but Pingomatic actually notifies a lot of other sites, including Google, so that one entry is fine and all I personally use.

You can find larger and ready-made ping lists created by other website owners if you want. Just search Google for "WordPress Ping List," find a list, and paste it into the box.

Don't forget to save if you make changes before moving to the next settings page.

5.3. Reading Settings

Latest posts vs. static page

If you have not published any WordPress Pages (pages, not posts) on your site, then you will see this:

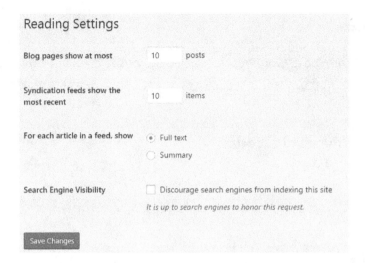

If you have published at least one page, then you will see this at the top of the settings:

The **"Your Homepage displays"** settings allow you to define what is shown on your homepage. If you have published a page, you can use that page as your homepage. Hence the reason these options are only available if you have a page published.

You have two options to use for the homepage on your site. You can select:

1. Your latest posts

2. A static page

If you select **a static page** as your homepage, then you will be required to select the pre-created WordPress page in the drop-down box.

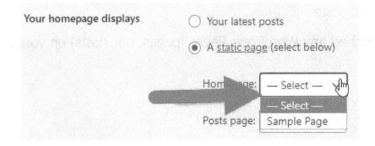

Next up on the Reading Settings is deciding how many posts to display on the archive pages (like category page, author page, etc.) and decide what information is shown in RSS feeds (something WordPress generates for your site).

Blog pages show at most	10	posts
Syndication feeds show the most recent	10	items
For each post in a feed, include	◉ Full text	
	○ Summary	

Your theme determines how content is displayed in browsers. Learn more about feeds.

Search engine visibility ☐ Discourage search engines from indexing this site

It is up to search engines to honor this request.

Save Changes

The default setting is 10, which means WordPress will show 10 posts on the homepage (if the homepage uses "latest posts," 10 on the category pages, and 10 on the author page, etc. If there are more than 10 posts to show, then the remainder will be added, in batches of 10, to additional pages, and you'll get a next/previous type navigation to move between them.

I would recommend you leave the **Blog pages show at most** set to 10.

Beneath that is the **syndication feeds show the most recent** option.

WordPress creates RSS feeds for your site. Your site will have a main feed, plus there will be feeds for category pages, tag pages, and so on. This setting tells WordPress how many items to include in the feed. With Google's Penguin algorithm looking at the over-optimization of inbound links, I'd limit the RSS feed to a maximum of 10. In the past, webmasters have included 100 items (or more), and that would mean any site that is displaying your RSS feed will contain 100 links back to it. Before Google Penguin, that was OK, but not now. Leave this number set at 10.

You now have to decide what the feed contains, i.e., all the content of your posts or just a summary of them. Select **Summary.** Otherwise, you are making it far too easy for scraper software tools to copy (steal) your content. These software tools monitor RSS feeds and strip the content out. Your content is then likely to be posted on one or more spammy sites around the internet, and that's not good.

Another reason to limit this to 10 is simply that RSS feeds are great for getting content indexed quickly. You only really need the last 10 items published on your site in the feed. Once these are indexed in the search engines, there is no need for them to still be in the feed. As more content is added to your site, they will scroll off the bottom of the feed and be replaced by newer content, ready for indexing.

The final option on this page is **search Engine Visibility**. When some people develop a website, they want it to be finished before the search engines come to spider the site. This option allows you to do just that. By checking the box, your website will tell the search engines to ignore it until you decide the time is right, and uncheck this option.

I have had dozens of students email me in the past asking why Google was not indexing their site. The reason in every case was that they had checked this box and forgotten they did so.

I recommend you leave this box unchecked from the start, that's unless you have good reason to not want the content indexed as you create it. As I add content to a website, I *want* Google to find and index it as soon as possible. If it sees new content being added regularly, it'll know the site is active and needs to be spidered more regularly to keep their index up to date. By leaving this option unchecked, you are encouraging the search engine spiders to crawl your site, and that's a good thing.

5.4 Discussion Settings

The Discussion Settings refer to the commenting system built into WordPress.

Google likes to see visitor interaction on a website, so this is an important part of your WordPress SEO. You'll want to keep the comments enabled.

At the top of these settings, you will see:

These boxes should all be left checked.

The first option means WordPress will try to send a notification to any blog you link to in your posts. This lets a site owner know you have linked to them and can sometimes result in a link back.

The second option is the first one in reverse. If someone links to your site, then WordPress will notify you so that you can see who's linking to you. This has been abused by spammers, and you will get a lot of false positives here, but it is worth checking out these notifications to see if someone is talking about you.

The final option simply tells WordPress to allow visitors to comment on your posts. This is what we want – visitor participation.

The **Other comment settings** section has a few more options:

Check the first box so that anyone leaving a comment must enter a name and an email address.

The second box should be unchecked unless you are creating some kind of membership site where people need to register to participate.

Leave the third box unchecked, too, unless there is a reason why you want to close comments on older posts. I personally like to keep comments open indefinitely, and if there is a post where I want to close them, I can do that on the **Edit Post** screen, just for that one post.

The fourth checkbox is there to keep your site GDPR compliant, so leave that checked. Search Google for GDPR if you want to know what that is.

The next checkbox will enable nested comments. This is something that not only makes the comments look better but more intuitive for your visitors. This is because replies to a specific comment will be nested under the original, and this, in turn, makes following the conversation much easier.

The next option allows you to spread comments across pages once you get over a certain number of remarks on the main post page. This is a good idea if your site gets a lot of comments because the more you have, the longer the page will take to load. If you anticipate a lot of comments, enable this option. You can also specify here whether you want comments to be shown with the oldest or newest first. I think it makes more sense to have older comments at the top. That way, the comments are chronological, but this is a personal preference.

Next on this page is the **E-mail me whenever** settings. Do you want to be notified when someone comments on a post? If so, make sure that option is checked. I recommend you check this so that you get instant notifications of any new comments posted on your site. This means you get to reply quickly. Fast responses to comments are important, and it makes the visitor feel that you care. Practicing good interaction means there's a much better chance the commenter will come back and visit your site again.

The second email option is to notify you when a comment is held for moderation. You can uncheck this because in a moment, we will tell WordPress to hold ALL comments for moderation, and we are already getting notified every time someone posts a comment anyway.

In the **Before a comment appears** section, check the first box, and uncheck the second.

NOTE: Don't be tempted to check the other box, which will auto-approve comments if the author has one already approved. Hackers have used this option in the past to get "approved" before posting a comment with malicious code embedded.

These settings will force ALL comments to appear in a moderation queue and will only go live on your site once you approve them.

This means the next couple of settings in the **Comment Moderation** section are irrelevant since ALL comments are now held for moderation. We can, therefore, ignore that section.

NOTE: Moderating comments might sound like a lot of work, but it is essential. If you have your site set up to auto-approve comments, your pages will end up full of spam remarks and possible security loopholes added by hackers trying to gain access. Needless to say, that would take a lot more time cleaning up than moderating comments.

The **"Comment Blacklist"** is a good way to fight spam. You can include email addresses, IP addresses, and certain words in the box. If a comment matches any of those lines, it is automatically marked as spam. If I end up getting a lot of spam comments from a particular IP address, I usually add that to this list as well.

You can search Google for a "WordPress comment blacklist," which will get you started. Just add one item per line, and save your changes when done.

The final section on the Discussion Settings relates to the use of "Avatars."

Avatars

An avatar is an image that follows you from weblog to weblog appearing beside your name when you comment on avatar enabled sites. Here you can enable the display of avatars for people who comment on your site.

Avatar Display

✔ Show Avatars

Maximum Rating

● G — Suitable for all audiences

○ PG — Possibly offensive, usually for audiences 13 and above

○ R — Intended for adult audiences above 17

○ X — Even more mature than above

An Avatar is a small image of the author. If the author of a comment has a Gravatar (http://gravatar.com/) assigned to the email address, and they use that same email to leave a comment, then that Gravatar is shown as their avatar.

I recommend you check **show Avatars**. I think this helps the comment section become more active since visitors to your site can see little photos of real people leaving remarks. Site visitors like to know who they are dealing with, a face behind the name as it were, so these images help instill confidence and help gain site credibility.

I would also recommend you check the G rating so the avatars on your site should be suitable viewing for all ages.

In the **Default** Avatar section, select **Blank**. Avatars take time to load, thus increasing the page load time. With blank selected, if a person does not have a Gravatar set up, no image is loaded for that person. If you leave it at the default "Mystery Person," that mystery person image will be loaded whenever someone leaves a comment and does not have a Gravatar set up.

5.5. Media Settings

While the settings here allow us to determine the default sizes of images in posts, I recommend you do that manually on a post-by-post basis at the time you create them.

Therefore, there are no specific settings in the Media Settings section that we need to change for SEO purposes.

5.6 Permalinks Settings

The Permalink settings are important because whatever you enter here will influence the way the URLs are displayed for the pages on your website.

The "Plain" WordPress setting will produce URLs like this:

mydomain.com/?p=123

The **?p=123** parameter in this URL is simply a call for the page with Page ID = 123. This is not very useful for visitors, it looks ugly, and it's certainly not helpful to search engines.

I recommend you use a permalink structure that contains at least the post name. This is the default setting.

◉ Post name   http://test.local/sample-post/

If your site has posts arranged in categories, why not include the categories as well? You can do this by selecting **Custom Structure** and selecting %category% %postname% from the available tags.

Here it is in my settings:

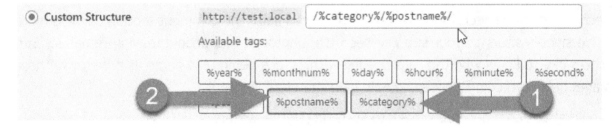

Now the URL of any page will include the category and filename of the post. A typical URL for a post might look like this:

mydomain.com/dog-breeds/alsatians

In this instance, the post filename is Alsatians, and the post is in the dog breeds category.

IMPORTANT:

With Google on the warpath over "Webspam," we need to be very careful about choosing the correct category names for our site, especially if we are including the category in the URL.

For example, if your site is called mydietreviews.com, and you had a category called **diets**, then the URL might look like this:

my**diet**reviews.com/**diets**/hollywood-**diet**/

This URL has the word **diet** in it three times. That could well be seen as keyword stuffing and should be avoided. If you think that this type of situation will arise on your site with the categories you have chosen, then play it safe and use the "post name" permalink structure instead.

At the bottom of the permalink settings, there are some optional choices:

To understand what these options do, I need to tell you how WordPress assigns the URL for category pages and tag pages.

Every category page will have the word **category** in the URL, and every tag page will have the word **tag** in the URL. Therefore, using the examples above, the category page URL would look like this:

mydietreviews.com/**category**/diets/

This category page will then show all the posts in the diets category.

Similarly, a tag page URL would look something like this:

mydietreviews.com/tag/fat-loss/

Any posts on your site that were tagged with the term **fat loss** would be listed on this page.

With that knowledge, let's go back to the "category base" and "tag base" settings.

If you leave these empty, then category and tag page URLs will be created as described above, with the word "category" or "tag" inserted into the URL.

If you prefer to use a different word than "category" or "tag" for these URLs, you can enter it in the "category base" and "tag base" settings.

For example, if you set the category base to **abracadabra**, then the category URL would become:

Before Panda and Penguin, category and tag bases were used to keyword stuff the URLs. Today, leave them blank as they will only get your site into trouble.

It is also possible to remove the word "category" altogether from category page URLs using a plugin that we'll look at later. This is not an option for tag page URLs.

5.7. Privacy

Finally, click on the **Privacy** link in the **Settings** menu.

The Privacy settings were introduced to help website owners get ready for GDPR compliance. If you don't know what that is, I recommend you research it a little. It is essentially a privacy law. One of the first steps in becoming compliant is to have a good privacy policy that visitors can read. This will tell them what information if any, your site collects and stores.

The Privacy options allow you to select an existing privacy policy if you already have one or create a new one.

WordPress created a draft privacy policy when you installed it, and if that is still available, you can use that, but it is a work in progress. Complete and publish your Privacy Policy if you haven't already.

As soon as your Privacy Policy is published, go back to the Privacy settings page and make sure your new privacy policy is selected:

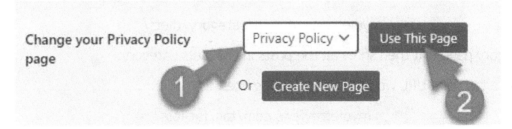

Click the **Use This Page** button.

6. Plugins

Before we look at the plugins, I need to mention that many are updated frequently, and their appearance can change a little as a consequence. That means the screenshots in this book may not be identical to what you see in your Dashboard. Most changes are minor, though, so you should still be able to set everything up properly, even if your plugin is a different version to the one that I am showing in this book.

What I am going to do in this section is get you to install certain plugins. We won't go through the configuration of each one just yet; we'll do that later in the book when we need to achieve certain SEO goals.

There are a few essential plugins to get your WordPress site ready for the search engines. I'll cover these first, and I recommend you install ALL three of them. I'll then list a few other plugins that you may find useful and explain what they do. You can hold off installing these until you know whether you will need them or not.

To install the plugins, login to the Dashboard, and from the left side column, go to Plugins -> Add New. You will see a search box & button. Enter the plugin names in the search box as I state them below, and then install and activate each one.

6.1. Essential Plugins

1. Yoast SEO

This is a comprehensive SEO plugin that will create a self-updating sitemap and allow us fine control over the SEO of the site.

Search for "Yoast SEO."

This is the one you are looking for, by Team Yoast:

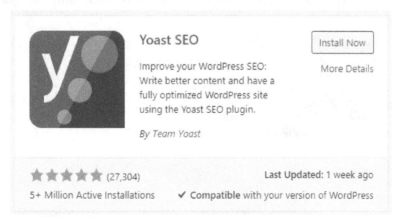

Click the Install now link, and once installed, activate the plugin.

2. W3 Total Cache

A caching plugin is essential because it speeds up your website. Page load speed, as mentioned previously, is an important part of SEO. Google likes fast loading pages, and once we have this plugin configured, your site should load several times faster than before.

NOTE: If you have a preferred caching plugin, you can use that instead,

Search for "W3 Total Cache."

This is the one you are looking for, by BoldGrid:

Install and activate the plugin.

The final essential plugin I recommend is to create dynamic sidebars on your website. I'll explain this in more detail later, but for now, you have a choice of two plugins.

3. Dynamic Sidebar Widgets

Option 1 is called **Dynamic Widgets**, and this allows us to create criteria for the display of our widgets. E.g., If you want a widget to only appear within a certain category of posts, you can do that.

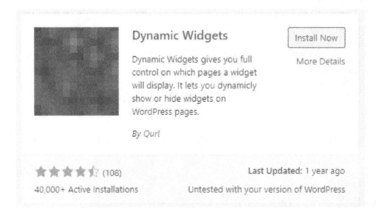

The Dynamic widgets plugin works on a widget-by-widget basis, so you can define rules for each widget independently.

Option 2 takes a different approach, allowing you to create entire sidebars and assign each one to different sections of your site. Be aware that with Gutenberg's introduction, sidebars are far less common now as Gutenberg encourages a full-width layout instead, putting the traditional sidebars at the bottom in the footer.

This one is called **Custom Sidebars:**

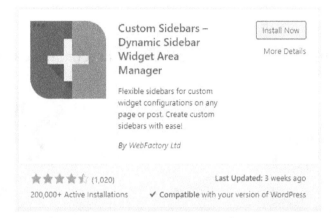

Whichever you choose is up to you and how you want to create your dynamic sidebars.

Install and activate your plugin of choice or both if you want to experiment before deciding which works better for your site.

That's it. Those are the essential plugins we need to set up for SEO purposes.

6.2 Non-essential Plugins

I won't be going into details on installing and configuring these non-essential plugins. I will just tell you what they do, and if you want to add them to your site, you can use the help documents that come with them should you need assistance setting them up.

Remember this, though. The more plugins you install on your site, the slower it will potentially load. Therefore, keep plugins to a minimum and only use the ones that you need.

1. YARPP

YARPP stands for **Yet Another Related Posts Plugin.** It creates a list of related posts dynamically for each post on your site. These posts can be automatically inserted after a post's content, or you can insert related posts as a widget, meaning you can place them into any widgetized area of your template, for example, a sidebar.

Search for "yarpp."

2. Ninja Forms Contact form

It's important that site visitors can contact you, so I recommend you install a contact form plugin.

The one I recommend is called Ninja Forms Contact Form.

3. UpdraftPlus

Updraft Plus has a free and premium version. For most people, the free version is all you'll need. This plugin will automatically backup your site on a schedule you choose. It will also help you restore your site from backup if you ever need to. UpdraftPlus can backup to S3, Dropbox, Google Drive, email, and other places.

Search for " updraftplus."

4. Broken Link Checker

If your site has a lot of outbound links to other websites (by the way, linking to authority sites within your niche is a good idea), then this plugin can check your outbound links and tell you if any are broken. Google doesn't like broken links on a site and may punish you if you have a lot of them. Therefore, this plugin can help ensure this does not become a problem.

Search for "broken link checker."

5. Grow by Mediavine

Having great content on your site is one thing, but getting people to see it is something else.

One of the ways people find a website is through search engines. If we rank well enough for a particular search term, the web searcher may land on our page.

Another way people can find our content is via social media channels. Places like Facebook and Twitter are good examples. To make this more likely, we need to install a social sharing plugin on the site. A social sharing plugin will add buttons to the website that allow people to share the content they are reading with their followers. Social sharing buttons make sharing easy, and therefore more likely.

There are several good social sharing plugins, and I do recommend you look around to find one that matches the design of your website. However, to get you started, I recommend you check out Grow by Mediavine:

6. Stop Spammers Spam Prevention

WordPress comes pre-installed with Akismet, a great anti-comment spam plugin. However, it is not free for commercial use. If you want a free plugin, try Stop Spammers Spam Prevention. Search for "stop spammers" and look for this one:

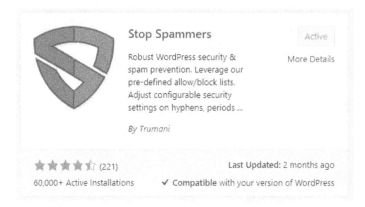

7. Pretty Links

This is a free plugin (there is a commercial version too, but the free version is all most people need). What this plugin does, is allow you to set up redirects on your site. Therefore, if you want to use an affiliate link on your page(s), you could set up a link like mydomain.com/affproduct, and this would redirect to the affiliate site. Why bother? If you don't know why you would want to do this, then you most probably don't need this plugin. One other nice feature is that it tracks clicks on all of the pretty links you set up, which can be very useful.

Search for "pretty links":

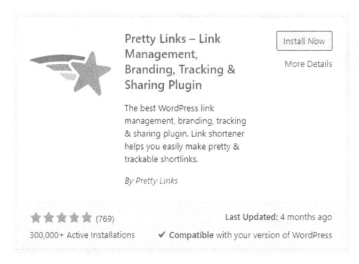

8. All in One Security & Firewall

This is a comprehensive, free security plugin that will protect your site against hackers. Search for "all in one security" and look for this plugin:

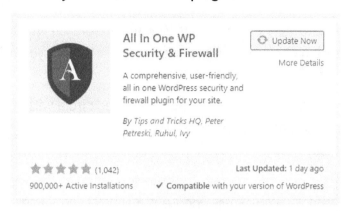

While it is beyond the scope of this book to show you how to set this up, I did record a quick start video to get you started. Go to ezseonews.com and search for **all in one security** to watch the video.

9. CI Backlinks

This plugin allows you to automate the internal linking of content across your site. It is a plugin I use on all of my websites because internal linking done manually is an almost impossible task. For example, when you add a new post to your website, you'd need to go and find all other posts that mention that topic so an internal link can be created. With this plugin, you set up the rules, and internal links are updated automatically as you add new content.

More details from https://ezseonews.com/wpseo

OK, that brings an end to my list of essential, and not so essential, plugins. Make sure you get the essentials installed before moving on. We'll be starting to configure them very soon.

7. Keeping WordPress Up to Date - WordPress & Plugins

You must always keep WordPress and plugins up to date. Hackers typically look for exploits in WordPress, so updates fix any known problems, thus keeping your website protected.

WordPress will auto-update minor versions of WordPress for you, making sure your site is always protected. Occasionally, when major versions are released, you will need to go in and manually update your installation.

If a WordPress or plugin update is available, you'll see a red circle with a number inside, next to the Updates menu on the Dashboard:

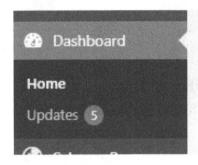

Click on **Updates** to be taken to the updates screen. This can have up to three sections. At the very top, if a WordPress update is available, you'll see an option to install it.

As you can see, mine is up to date:

You have the latest version of WordPress. Future security updates will be applied automatically.

If you need to re-install version 5.3.2, you can do so here:

Re-install Now

Under that, if plugins are available for updates, you'll see them here.

Simply check the plugins you want to update, and then click the **Update Plugins** button.

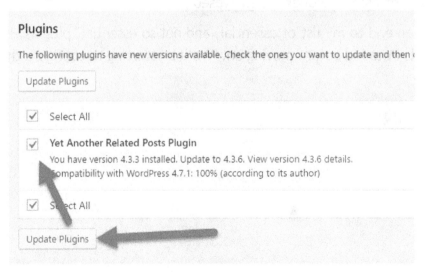

At the bottom of the page, if a theme has an update, you should see it listed here, too (though that will depend on the theme and where you got it from). Again, check the theme(s) you want to update, and click the **Update Themes** button.

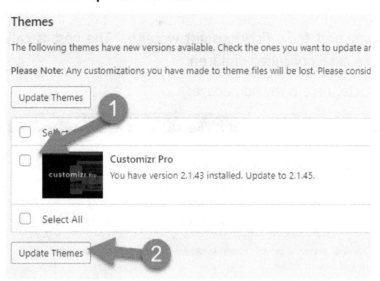

8. Duplication on Category, Tag & Other Archive Pages

As mentioned at the beginning of this book, these pages are the root of many SEO problems. Let me show you an example of this.

I've created a dummy post for a fictitious gift website. The post is called **Gift ideas for children**, and it's in a category called **children**.

After posting the article, here is my homepage:

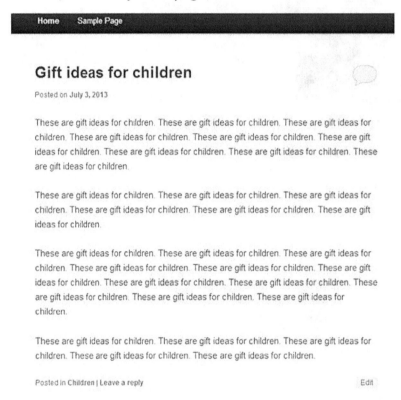

The title of the post is a hyperlink that will open a page that contains an exact copy of the article. That means we now have two identical copies of the same post, but that's only the tip of the iceberg.

Look at the screenshot above under the title where it says Posted on July 3, 2013. That date is a hyperlink to the date archive. Clicking on it takes me to a page that shows all posts that were published on that date. Here it is:

Gift ideas for children

These are gift ideas for children. These are gift ideas for children. These are gift ideas for children. These are gift ideas for children. These are gift ideas for children. These are gift ideas for children. These are gift ideas for children. These are gift ideas for children. These are gift ideas for children.

These are gift ideas for children. These are gift ideas for children. These are gift ideas for children. These are gift ideas for children. These are gift ideas for children. These are gift ideas for children.

These are gift ideas for children. These are gift ideas for children. These are gift ideas for children. These are gift ideas for children. These are gift ideas for children. These are gift ideas for children. These are gift ideas for children. These are gift ideas for children. These are gift ideas for children. These are gift ideas for children. These are gift ideas for children. These are gift ideas for children.

The same full post again.

Go back to the homepage screenshot. See at the bottom of the post where it says **Posted in children**. **Children** is the category, and the word children is a hyperlink. If I click that, it takes me to the children category page:

Gift ideas for children

Posted on July 3, 2013

These are gift ideas for children. These are gift ideas for children. These are gift ideas for children. These are gift ideas for children. These are gift ideas for children. These are gift ideas for children. These are gift ideas for children. These are gift ideas for children. These are gift ideas for children.

These are gift ideas for children. These are gift ideas for children. These are gift ideas for children. These are gift ideas for children. These are gift ideas for children. These are gift ideas for children.

These are gift ideas for children. These are gift ideas for children. These are gift ideas for children. These are gift ideas for children. These are gift ideas for children. These are gift ideas for children. These are gift ideas for children. These are gift ideas for children. These are gift ideas for children. These are gift ideas for children. These are gift ideas for children. These are gift ideas for children.

These are gift ideas for children. These are gift ideas for children. These are gift ideas for

That page also contains the full post.

The duplication doesn't stop there. WordPress has also created an author page. If I go to the author page:

Once again, we have yet another duplicated copy of the same article.

But wait, there's more! What if I added a few tags to the post? Here I've added four tags to this demo article:

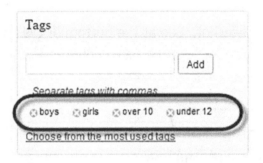

The tags are boys, girls, over 10 & under 12. These are supposed to help classify gift ideas. However, WordPress creates a page for each of these tags, and guess what?

I'll give you a clue by showing you one of the four tag pages:

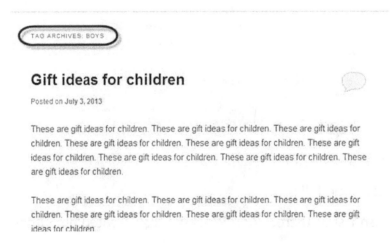

Yes, that's right. The full article is published on each of the four tag pages too.

So how many times does this one post appear on the site? Well, assuming I haven't missed one or two copies (something which is quite possible), we have the following:

Homepage, post page, category page, date archive, author page, and four tag pages. That's nine copies of the same article. And that happens with every article you publish on your site.

Now, do you see why WordPress desperately needs to be SEO'd? This type of duplication can kill your rankings in Google.

If you are starting to have palpitations, thinking you have made the wrong decision choosing WordPress, relax. I'll walk you through it step by step. It isn't so difficult to solve these problems once you know how.

9. Menus & Site Navigation

Visitors like a site with good navigation, and Google likes a site that keeps its visitors happy. Of course, there is more to it than that. Good navigation on a site will help the search engines find and even categorize your content.

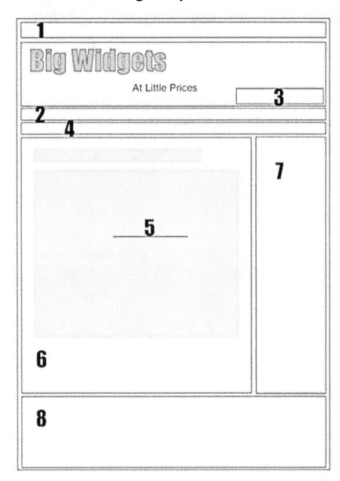

On a website, there are various places where navigation can appear. These typically include:

1.   A menu above the site logo.

2.   A menu below the site logo.

3.   A search box in the same area as the site logo, often off to the right.

4.   Breadcrumb navigation underneath the page header but above the web page opening header.

5.   Links to other pages within the body of the content, as in-context links.

6.   After the content of the page, maybe as **Related Articles** or **You may also be interested in** type lists.

7.   A menu in the left and/or right sidebar.

8.   A menu in the page footer.

Where you insert your navigation may be determined by your choice of WordPress theme. For example, some themes offer positions 1 or 2, but not both. Others offer both positions. And some may offer two navigation menus in position 2, but none in position 1.

As for the search box, this can appear in the logo area or the sidebar. I've even seen them in page footers. Therefore, this diagram is only a rough guide.

Before we look at how to create the various forms of navigation in WordPress, let me mention one thing. Create your navigation for human visitors, not search engines. That means using the most logical and aesthetically pleasing links in the menu. Do not, under any circumstances, stuff keywords into your navigation menus and links.

For example, if you had a website about prom dresses and had sections on your site to various brands of prom dress, you might be tempted to use something like:

- PacificPlex Prom Dresses
- Ever-Pretty Prom Dresses
- Moonar Prom Dresses
- Hot from Hollywood Prom Dresses
- US Fairytailes Prom Dresses

Notice the repetition of the words **Prom Dresses**. Why do you think some webmasters do this? Is it to help their visitors? Well, considering the whole site is about prom dresses, I'd assume not. This is done purely for the search engines for two reasons:

1. In this menu, the phrase **prom dresses** appears five times in the hope that the page would rank better for that term. In the good old days of pre-2011 SEO, this would have worked. Today it's more likely to get you a Penguin penalty.

2. Each item in the menu will link to a page on the site. That link uses anchor text (the text you see). In this type of menu, the keyword-stuffed anchor text is there as an attempt to boost the rankings of the page the link points to for its anchor text phrase. Say if this site had 100 pages, each using the same prom dress menu. This means each of the five pages in the menu would have 100 links pointing to them. That's 100 of the same anchor texts. Again, pre-2011, this worked. Today it does not, and this tactic will come back to bite you (or do Penguins nip?).

TIP: Look at the SEO on your site. If you cannot say with 100% that you have done it in your visitor's best interests, then get rid of it. This goes for site navigation, content, and internal linking between pages, etc.

OK, with that said, how do you implement navigation into WordPress?

Well, there are several different ways.

You can use plugins. You can also use the menu system built into WordPress.

In many cases, you will know which links you want in a navigation area. These links are usually fixed and rarely change. In this instance, I recommend you use the menu system built into WordPress.

On other occasions, you might want a list of the most recent posts or posts related specifically to the current one. These menus are constantly changing as new content gets added to the site and are therefore best handled with plugins.

9.1. Recommended Navigation

Let me make the recommendations first, and then I'll show you how to implement them.

To start (you can add or change this later), I suggest that you have the following four navigation features:

1. **A "legal" menu:** Either above or below the site logo or in the footer, where there are links to your legal pages. That's the Contact, Privacy, Disclaimers, and so forth. These links should be **nofollowed**, and the actual legal pages should be set to **noindex**, **Follow** and **No Archive**. This menu should also have a dofollow link to the "About Us" page, which is often one of the most visited pages on a website.

2. **A search box:** If your theme supports a search box in the header area, you might want it there. However, I prefer a search box at the top of the sidebar (right or left, whichever I use).

3. **A main navigation menu:** In the logo area or sidebar (right or left) that links to the main sections of your website (the main categories and/or most important pages).

4. **Sidebar dynamic menus:** Each category (or main section) of your site should have a different navigation menu in the sidebar. Google likes dynamic menus that change depending on where a visitor is. For example, if you are in the mountain bike section of a site, the main navigation menu should be related to mountain bikes. If you are in the road bike section, the main navigation menu relates to road bikes.

Personally, the type of sites I build also benefit from a **related posts** section, either after the main content of a post or in the sidebar (done using the YARPP plugin). However, it depends on the type of site you build, so this may not suit your particular project. I also implement internal linking between the posts on the site using context-sensitive links (this is done using the **C.I. Backlinks** plugin I recommended in the non-essential plugins earlier). The internal linking of posts on a site is something that most of the big players do (see Wikipedia, for example), and it does help your pages get indexed and rank better.

9.2. Implementing the Four Main Navigation Features

Let's look at the **legal menu** first.

9.2.1. Implementing Legal Menus

If you log in to the Dashboard and go to Appearance -> Menus, you'll be able to create a menu that contains links to your legal pages.

I always give menus a name that will explain what the menu is for, so in this case, I'd call it "legal."

You do need to make some of the links in this menu "nofollow," so let me show you how to do that.

Pull down the Screen Options (top right of the Dashboard), and make sure that **Link Relationship (XFN)** is checked.

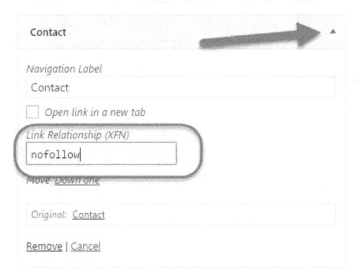

You can now expand the items in your menu:

Type the word **nofollow** into the link relationship box.

Repeat this for all your legal pages, and don't forget to save your menu.

Once you have the menu saved, you can then insert it into your theme.

At the top of the screen, you should see the **Manage Locations** tab:

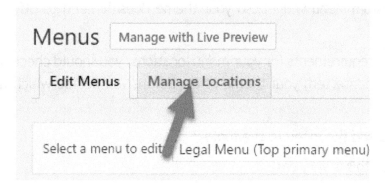

Click on that to open up the locations screen. What you'll see depends on the theme you are using. The following is for the Twenty Fourteen theme:

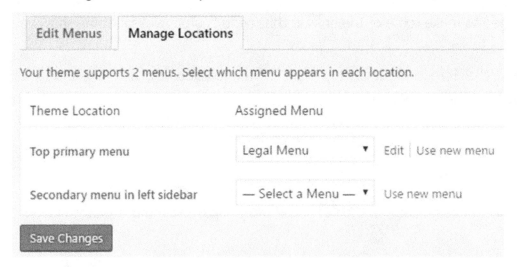

You can see that this theme has two areas allocated for menus. The **top primary menu** and the **secondary menu in the left sidebar**. You can use the drop-down boxes to select a menu for each location. If you are unsure where on your site one of these locations is found, add a menu and visit the site. You'll see where the menu has been added.

Here is another theme:

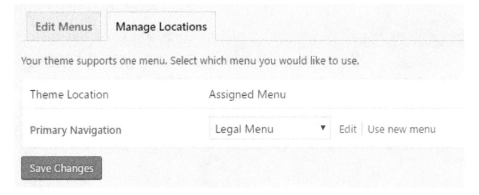

This one only allocates one area for a menu. You can easily add a menu to the sidebar of any theme using a Custom Menu widget, so your theme doesn't need to offer this location by default.

If you have specific requirements for your menu locations, you should check how many menus (and where they are inserted) your theme offers before you decide which theme to use for your site.

OK, so how do you add the menu to the footer?

With some themes, this is very easy.

Go to the Appearance -> Widgets screen.

On the right of the screen, you will see the areas that can accept widgets. For example, the Twenty Seventeen theme offers me three locations for widgets:

The sidebar and two footers. If your theme has two footer areas, one is likely to be the left half of the footer and one the right half. Some themes offer three footer widgets, so the footer is split into equal thirds.

On the left, you should be able to see the Custom Menu widget.

Simply drag the Custom Menu Widget into the Footer Widget area (or sidebar if that is where you want your menu), and then select the legal menu:

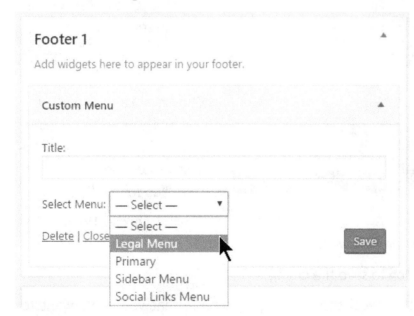

Congratulations, you've just added your legal menu to the footer area of your site. Go and check it out.

All links will be nofollow because we set that up in the actual menu settings.

There is one other task we need to do. That is to make sure our legal pages are set up so that they are **noindex**, **Follow**, and **No Archive**. Fortunately, this is easy with the Yoast SEO plugin we installed earlier.

Go to each of your legal pages in turn and open them in the editor (Pages -> All Pages, then click on the title of the page in the list).

The Yoast SEO plugin has added a section to all post/page edit screens. Look for the section with the title **Yoast SEO.**

We want to open the **Advanced** section at the bottom:

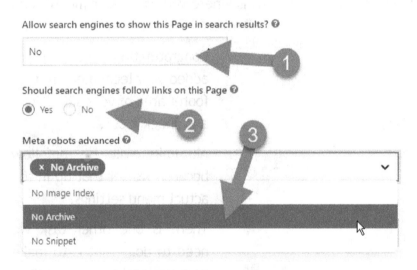

Select **No** from the "Allow search engines to show this Page in search results" drop-down box. This makes the page noindex.

Choose **Yes** from the "Should search engines follow links on this page?." This makes the links on the page "do follow."

Finally, choose **No Archive** from the "Meta robots advanced" drop-down box.

Now click the page's **Update** button to save the changes.

Repeat this procedure for all other legal pages (and pages/posts that you don't want to appear in the search engines).

OK, now you have a legal menu on your site, with links to these pages set as nofollow, and the pages themselves set as noindex, noarchive. These settings will prevent Google from indexing pages that are not important to your site and thus stop valuable Page Rank from flowing to these pages, meaning more link juice for your important content. The fact that links from these pages can still be followed means better spidering of your site.

9.2.2. Implementing a Search Box

WordPress comes with a search widget, so you can start by using that. They aren't very good, so I recommend you eventually switch to using a Google custom search (search Google for instructions when you are ready), but the WordPress search feature will do to get you started.

Simply drag the **search** widget to the widgetized area where you want it to. Some themes will offer you a **Header Right** option. This will insert a widget into the right-hand side of the logo area. You can drag the search box widget there if you want to. Alternatively, drag it to the top of the main or default sidebar.

You can enter a title for the widget if you like. The title will then appear right above the search box. However, the title isn't really necessary. Here is a search box inserted into my sidebar in the Twenty Seventeen theme without a title:

It looks great as it is!

9.2.3. Main Site Navigation Menu

The main site navigation should link to the main areas of your site (pages, sections, or categories). These links should all be dofollow to help spread link juice around the site.

If you don't want to use the default menu locations for your main site navigation, you can insert that into the sidebar if you wish. Drag and drop a **Custom Menu** widget into the area you want your main navigation to appear, and select your main site menu. However, I do think the best option for main site navigation is across the top of your site, just under the logo, so I recommend you insert it there if your theme allows.

9.2.4. Dynamic Navigation Menus

The last type of navigation I suggested you use is dynamic navigation. These are menus that change depending on the area of the site a visitor is reading. We used the example of a bike website earlier. If someone is browsing the mountain bike section, the "dynamic" menu should show further options related to mountain bikes. When reading content on road bikes, the dynamic menus should offer further road bike content. After all, if someone wants to switch from mountain bikes to road bikes, the main navigation at the top will allow them to do that.

9.2.4.1. Creating Dynamic Navigation Menus with Dynamic Widgets

To achieve dynamic menus, we need the **Dynamic Widgets** or **Custom Sidebars** plugin that I recommended earlier. If you want to see how to use Custom Sidebars, go to my site at ezseonews.com and search for Custom Sidebars. I have a tutorial there.

In this book, I'll quickly go over the Dynamic Widgets plugin. When this is installed, EVERY widget you add in the Appearance -> Widgets section of the dashboard has a new feature:

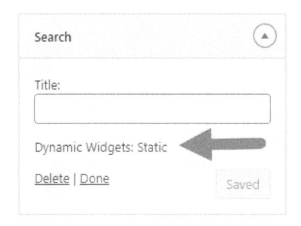

See **Dynamic Widgets: Static**?

That word **static** is a hyperlink that takes you to the settings for the widget. Click on it, and you get to specify exactly where on the site you want the widget to appear.

The default setting is static, which means the widget appears on every page & post of the entire site, but you can change the default. Say you have a navigation menu that you only want to appear on the homepage.

Click on the "static" link to be taken to the configuration screen.

This opens up a large page of options.

Each of these horizontal bars will open up if you click on them.

Since we only want the menu to appear on the homepage, the first thing we need to do is click the link at the top of these options: **Set all options to 'No.'**

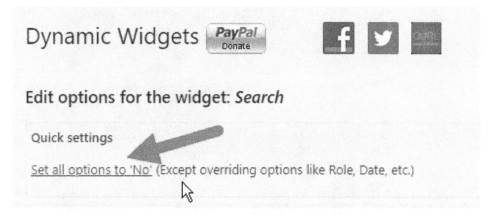

If we now click on any one of these bars, it will expand, showing us that it is set to no.

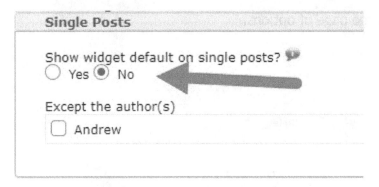

This means the widget will not appear anywhere on the site. We need to fix this by opening up the homepage options (called **Front Page** in this plugin) and select **Yes**.

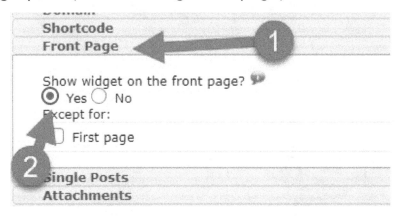

Now, don't forget to save the settings by clicking the **save** button at the bottom. This will then return you to the widgets area of the Dashboard.

If you look at the Navigation Menu widget, you'll see that additional information I told you about is now listed in the Dynamic Widgets section:

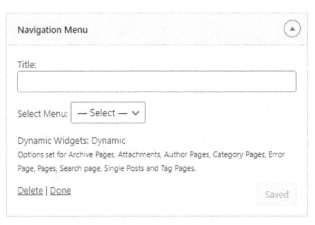

The word **static** now reads **Dynamic**, and we can see that the options have been set for various pages on the site.

If you check your site, you will find the main navigation menu only appears on the homepage.

To create dynamic menus for each specific area of your site, you need to set up the menu in the Appearance -> Menu section.

For example, if you have five categories on your site, set up five Custom Menus and include the most relevant menu items for each category.

Next, add all of these custom menus to the sidebar, and then go into them, one by one, and change the settings for where they should appear on your site.

Let's assume I want the custom menu to appear only in the **Hot from Hollywood** category (that's the category page plus any posts in that category).

Step one will be to click the link to set all options to **No**, just as we did for the homepage. Next, we need to change two settings.

The first is in the **Category Pages** settings:

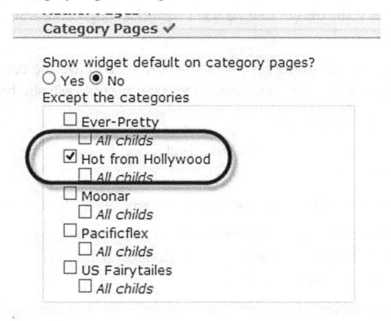

Select **No** at the top, and then check the **Hot from Hollywood** checkbox. This may sound counter-intuitive, but read the information on the plugin settings screen. We are checking the Hot from Hollywood category so that it will be the exception. We don't want the widget to appear on category pages EXCEPT for the one(s) that are checked.

OK, once saved, that will show the menu on the **Hot from Hollywood** category page. We also need to make it appear on the posts within that category, so we have to set the **single Posts** options.

Single Posts ✓

Show widget default on single posts? 💬
○ Yes ◉ No

Except the author(s)
☐ Maria

Except the categories
☐ Ever-Pretty
  ☐ All childs
☑ Hot from Hollywood
  ☑ All childs
☐ Moorlai
  ☐ All childs
☐ Pacificflex
  ☐ All childs
☐ US Fairytailes
  ☐ All childs

Again, we select **No** at the top because we don't want this widget appearing on posts, except the ones we check

The **Hot from Hollywood** category is selected, but you also have the option to check *All childs*, which will mean any **Hot from Hollywood** sub-categories will also have this menu.

OK, once done, save your changes.

The menu will only appear on the **Hot from Hollywood** category page AND all the posts within that category.

Repeat this process for each dynamic menu you are creating for your website.

I recommend you read the documentation for the dynamic widgets plugin and play around with it. As you explore the other settings, you will discover it offers an enormous level of control over widget placement on your site.

Using the techniques shown in this chapter, you can easily create custom sidebars and custom footers with any type of widget in any widgetized area.

This is the easiest way to create dynamic navigation systems on your website. Don't forget, besides navigation systems, you can also serve up custom adverts, custom subscription boxes, custom videos, etc., and all on different sections of the site.

10. Comment System

The comment systems and how to integrate them into your site is an important yet often over-looked piece of the on-site SEO puzzle.

The comments on your site are VERY important. A lot of comments tell visitors that your site is busy. If it's busy, then it's likely to be trusted by more people. If it's trusted, it will do better in Google too.

However, all of this is dependent on having good quality comments. Comments need to add to the conversation that has gone before them. Put more specifically, do the comments add to the original article, either by way of an opinion, additional information, or a question? Another good type of comment is when a visitor replies to someone else's remarks, but again, only if those replies are adding to the conversation. These are the types of comments you need to try and get on your site.

When a website is new, it's all too easy to approve poor comments just to make the site look visited. Don't do it! Never approve a comment *unless* it adds something to the post topic and conversation already on-going; that's if there are other comments, of course.

Typical comments you shouldn't approve include "Well done!," or "Great post." Even "Thanks for writing about this topic in a way I can understand." Although the latter might sound sincere, it adds absolutely nothing to the conversation because there is no reference to the topic in question.

Get used to approving only the best comments. Even if you don't get very many to begin with (which is quite possible), great comments add value to the overall visitor experience of your website. Or, to put it another way, a website full of poor & spammy comments will put your visitors off, and they won't have much confidence in you or the credibility of your site.

11. RSS Feeds

WordPress automatically creates several RSS feeds for your site.

You can access the main feed for your site by adding **/feed** to the end of your domain URL.

The feed for my SEO website is **ezSEONews.com/feed**.

We set up the RSS feed earlier to show just 10 posts and only the title and excerpts of those. Therefore, the main feed will show the last 10 posts you published on your site.

WordPress also creates several other RSS feeds for:

1. Comments.
2. Post-specific feeds.
3. Categories.
4. Tags.
5. Authors.
6. Search feeds.

I won't go into details showing you how to find all of these feeds. If you are interested, you can read the WordPress codex article on this topic:

https://wordpress.org/support/article/wordpress-feeds/

From an SEO point of view, feeds are interesting. For example, there are some RSS feed submission services where you can get backlinks to your site by submitting your feed(s). Whenever you add fresh content, these feeds get updated, linking back to the new page. In terms of helping pages rank higher, these types of links won't help at all, but they can get your new content indexed a lot quicker. What I would suggest here is not to overdo this type of submission. Pick maybe one or two of the top RSS feed sites, and submit your main site feed to each.

One thing I like to use feeds for is adding a "recent posts" section to my site's sidebar or footer. WordPress comes with an RSS widget, and all you need to do is supply the feed URL for it to work.

For example, on my SEO site, I have a category for all "blog posts." I can grab the feed URL for that category:

https://ezseonews.com/category/blog/feed/

I can then add it to an RSS widget:

The feed will then show wherever I add this widget:

If I only want the feed to appear on certain areas of the site, I can set this up using the dynamic widget or sidebar options.

The widget would then display the 10 most recent posts from that section in my sidebar.

Best of all is that as new content is added to the site, the feed is updated, and so is the list in my sidebar.

This has a couple of benefits:

1.   You can highlight other recent articles in a given category.

2.   From an SEO perspective, this is good because you have inter-linking relevant articles, each reinforcing the theme of your pages and providing spiderable links to the other articles in the silo.

12. Google Authorship & WordPress User Profiles

Google is always updating its algorithm. There are hundreds of minor updates every year, with some major ones sprinkled in between. In the last couple of years, we've had to contend with Panda, Penguin, and then Penguin 2.0 (which was a major upgrade to the original). All of these updates have been necessary because Google has faced a constant battle with webmasters trying to game the system; that is, webmasters who want their content to rank #1 in the Google search results pages.

We all want to be ranked #1 for various search phrases - obviously - but we don't all deserve these top slot(s). Google has a problem with webmasters that try to force their content to the top of the first page. Google wants total control. They need to be able to decide which content deserves to be at the top and not leave that up to webmasters, who can and do, try all manner of techniques to get these valuable positions.

One of the most abused SEO techniques over the years has been link building. The general principle has always been more is better. Webmasters have always considered link building to be a safe practice because you cannot control who links to your site. Google themselves even told us once that links could not hurt a site's rankings.

Eventually, though, Google snapped. As things stand today, poor incoming (and outgoing) links can now hurt your site. To help webmasters fix link problems, Google introduced the disavow tool. You can use this to list those links pointing at your site which you do not approve of. This now means that site owners have full control over the links to their pages, signifying Google has shifted the responsibility of bad links away from their algorithm and onto the webmaster. In other words, if you have bad links pointing to your site, it is *your* fault as far as Google is concerned.

While the Google vs. Webmasters battle has raged on all these years, Google has constantly been looking for other signals they could use to help them better rank web pages. The holy grail of signals would be one that webmasters could not manipulate to their advantage.

12.1. Google Authorship

Several years ago, Google introduced "Google Authorship" linked to Google+ profile pages in search results as a way to connect a piece of content with its true author. Authors could see their photo appearing in SERPs, and anyone clicking the image would be taken to the author's profile page. However, that has since been removed from the search results.

I'm not sure why Google stopped using authorship, but I do think you need to take all the measures you can to be credited as the true author of your site content. For that reason, I want to talk a little bit about Gravatars and author biographies.

12.2. Gravatars & the Author Bio on Your Site

Everyone likes to see who they are dealing with, and in the more anonymous online world, it helps build your brand. Putting a face behind the name adds trust and credibility to your site(s) too. I, therefore, recommend you use a real photo of yourself and include it in an "author bio" after every post on your site. You should use the same photo when you leave comments on other websites, too.

The first step in achieving this is to sign up for a Gravatar:

https://en.gravatar.com/

When you get there, you'll see a button to "Create your own Gravatar." Click on that and follow the instructions. Gravatars are closely linked to an email address. When you leave a comment on another website, that website will check to see if the email address used in the comment has an associated Gravatar. If it is, that Gravatar image will be used with your comment.

Therefore, you need to enter the same email address that you've set up in your WordPress Dashboard.

Just follow the on-screen instructions to set up your Gravatar.

Once your account has been set up, you can upload an image and connect your email address to that photo. Try to use this same photo of yourself in all promotional activities. This will help brand you as the expert wherever you contribute, and people will start to recognize your face.

NOTE: You can add multiple email addresses to your Gravatar account, so if you control lots of sites or have many email addresses, you can assign the same (or a different) image to every email you'd like a Gravatar for.

Once this is set up, if you leave comments on blogs that have Gravatars enabled (btw, most of them do), then your image will show up next to your comments (assuming you entered the same email address when submitting them). Some forums also use Gravatars for images, so as you can see, we have multiple ways to brand ourselves and build trust around the web.

12.2.1. Author Bio Boxes

To set up the author bio on your posts, login to the dashboard and go to the Users -> Your profile page.

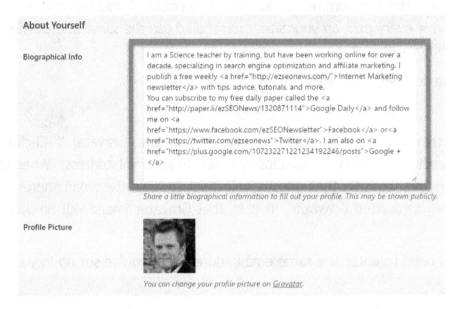

Under the profile picture, you should see your Gravatar!

In the **Biographical Info** box, enter the bio that you want to appear for each post on your site.

If your theme inserts an author bio box after posts, this should then appear after each post like this:

If your theme does not natively support author bio boxes, then you can add these using a plugin instead. Search the plugin repository for "author bio box," and there will be a number you can try. For example, this one:

Author Bio Box

Display a box with the author's biography in your WordPress

By claudiosanches

Install Now

More Details

★★★★★ (16)

6,000+ Active Installations

Last Updated: 6 months ago

Untested with your version of WordPress

I set this plugin up with my information on a site using the Twenty Seventeen (which does not natively add an author bio box after posts). This is the result:

Andy Williams

I am a Science teacher by training, but have been working online for over a decade, specializing in search engine optimization and affiliate marketing. I publish a free weekly Internet Marketing newsletter with tips, advice, tutorials, and more. You can subscribe to my free daily paper called the Google Daily and follow me on Facebook or Twitter. I am also on Google +

That's not bad at all!

13. Robots.txt File

The robots.txt file is a plain text file that contains various instructions for the search engines and other bots visiting your site. It includes details on specific folders and files that the search engines should or should not spider.

For example, you could tell the search engines to ignore all files within a specific folder on your server.

If you know you need a robots.txt file to restrict crawler access to your site, then you can ignore the following advice.

A few years ago, a good robots.txt file was important for a WordPress site, and Google expected one. Today, Google says you can use one if you want, but it prefers you don't. To properly spider and index a WordPress website, Google needs access to most folders and files on your server.

Therefore, I recommend you don't bother with a robots.txt file. The only reason I include a section on the robots.txt file in this book is that I get asked about it so often by my WordPress students.

If you do have one for your site and want to keep it, this is the full robots.txt I recommend:

#My robots.txt file

User-agent: *

This command simply means that the commands that follow should be applied to all crawlers. Since there are no other commands, crawlers are free to crawl without restriction.

14. WWW or No WWW?

Some websites use the www. prefix, and others don't. Google treats these as different URLs, so www.mysite.com is different from mysite.com.

If you have a site that uses subdomains, then using www. Makes sense.

If your site does not have subdomains, then it doesn't matter whether you choose www or non-www.

However, in both cases, you must be consistent. All links on your site or pointing to your site MUST use the same version.

You, therefore, need to decide which way you want your site's URL to be displayed.

Once WordPress is installed, visit your homepage by typing in the www. version of the domain. See what WordPress does by default. More often than not, your URL will be re-directed to the non-WWW version of the web page.

My advice is to use whatever WordPress shows you by default unless you have a good reason to want the other version.

If you do decide to change from one to another, be aware that you could break your site if you do it incorrectly. This change affects:

1. The URL your visitors will see.
2. The URL you use to login to the dashboard.
3. The functioning of your site's internal links and all external links pointing at your site.

If you do decide to change, the easiest way to do this is to log in to your WordPress Dashboard and go to the Settings -> General screen

WordPress Address (URL)   https://ezseonews.com

Site Address (URL)   https://ezseonews.com

Enter the address here if you want your site home page to be differe

Edit these fields for your preferred format and save. I recommend you now log out and back in again, just to test everything is still working.

15. Pages Versus Posts

When you want to add written content to your site, you have two options. You can either create a **Page or a Post. In terms of adding/editing, these two are very similar, but they are actually quite different in terms of function.**

This may sound confusing to people who are new to WordPress (or maybe even new to website building). After all, isn't a post on your site a page? Doesn't a page on your site contain a post?

For some reason, WordPress creators decided to name these two types of content "posts" and "pages," and it does cause confusion. However, you do need to understand the basic differences between them when it comes to building your site.

Since WordPress was originally designed as a blogging platform (i.e., to help build websites that were constantly updated with posts about whatever was going on in that blogger's life), posts were designed for these regular, chronological updates.

WordPress **posts** are *date-dependent and chronological,* and this separates them from **pages** that are date-independent and not really related to any other piece of content on the site.

Posts were originally designed to be ordered by date. A post you created yesterday should logically appear lower down the page than a post you make today. Newer posts are inserted at the top of the page, and older posts are pushed off the bottom. If you think back to the WordPress reading settings, we saw that the default homepage of a WordPress site shows posts in this manner.

A typical blog will be structured this way. Let's look at an example.

Suppose you were keeping a blog about your weight loss program. On day one, you weighed in at 210lb, so you write about that and what you have done for the day to help with your diet. Each day you write a new entry as a kind of personal journey on your weight loss progress.

When someone comes to your site, they see the daily posts in chronological order. This means visitors to your blog can follow your story logically and see how your diet is working out for you.

This type of chronology is not possible with pages (well, it is, but it takes a lot of effort plus plugins to achieve, so why bother?). Pages do not have any defined order, though they can have a hierarchy of parent and child pages.

OK, so date-dependency is one important difference between WordPress posts and pages. What else?

Well, posts can be categorized, pages cannot (at least not without plugins).

Suppose you were creating a site about exercise equipment. You might have a series of reviews on different treadmills, another set of reviews on exercise bikes, and so on.

Using posts allows us to categorize our content into relevant groups. If I had ten reviews of various weight loss programs, I could create a category on my site called weight loss programs and add all ten reviews to this category by writing them as posts.

Putting related content into the same category makes sense from a human visitor's point of view, but also from the point of view of a search engine. If someone were on your site reading a review of the Hollywood Diet, it would be easy to use features of WordPress posts to highlight other reviews in the same category. This can be done with posts on autopilot, but it is a much more manual process if you tried doing the same thing with pages.

Posts can also be tagged with related words and phrases.

Tags are an additional way to group and categorize your content. We'll discuss tags later, but for now, realize that they can be used to categorize your content further to help your visitors and the search engines make sense of your project.

It is possible to create tags for pages as well, but once again, only with plugins. As a rule, we try not to use plugins unless they are essential, as they can slow down the loading time of a website and possibly add security vulnerabilities if they are not well maintained by their creators.

Another great feature of posts is that they can have **Excerpts**. These are short descriptions of the article that can be used by themes and plugins to create a Meta description tag or a description of the article in a list of related articles. For example, below is a related posts section (created using a plugin) on one of my websites. It shows excerpts being used for the post descriptions:

Related Posts

1. What Are Tags in WordPress

   Learn about tags in WordPress, how they differ from Categories, and when to use them. Tags are a simple, highly-effective way for webmasters to organise and enhance web content.

2. How to Add Custom Hyperlinks to Your WordPress Gallery Images

   You can add custom links to your gallery or single images in WordPress. This step-by-step tutorial shows how to quickly add and edit custom links from the Post Edit screen.

3. How to Add WordPress Menu Items Without Linking to a Page

   A quick how-to Guide on how to add non-linking titles for Dropdown Menus in WordPress. Create neat menus for posts and pages to improve site navigation for your visitors.

Another important feature of posts is that they appear in your site's RSS feed. Remember, we talked about how important RSS feeds are earlier in the book. RSS feeds highlight the most recent posts, but pages are not included.

When to Use Posts and When to Use Pages

OK, this is the million-dollar question that I get asked a lot!

This will depend on the type of website you want to build. For a lot of company websites, using pages for most of the content makes sense, like this:

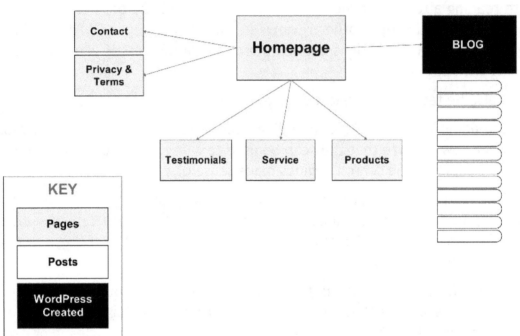

In this model, the company site uses WordPress "pages" for all of the main important content that they want to convey to visitors. That includes Homepage, Contact, Privacy, Terms, Testimonials, Services, and Products. These pieces of content are all isolated and unrelated to one another. The date of publishing is not important, so they are date-independent, and they don't need to be on the company RSS feed.

The company site also has a blog, and in this model, the blog is built with posts. From the point of view of this company, what features of posts make them ideal for the company blog?

The fact that posts are chronological? Sure. That means the company can post product updates, with the latest announcements at the top! The fact that these blog posts will end up in the company feed will help spread the news.

What about a site that is intended to be a blog? What would that look like?

I would suggest this model is ideal for a blog:

A Typical Blog

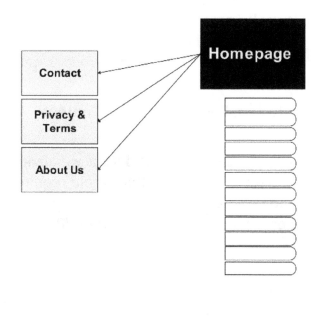

In this model, the homepage would be created by WordPress and just display the last ten or so blog posts. Newer posts would appear at the top, while older posts fall off the bottom (and on to page 2).

The blog posts would all use the power of WordPress "posts" (chronology and feed), while pages would only be used for Contact, Privacy, Terms, and an About Us page.

But WordPress has even more up its sleeves. The properties of posts, especially the ability to categorize posts, allow us to be very creative in site design. The main type of website I usually build is a completely different model from the two we've just seen. It uses elements of both a blog and a business site but throws categories into the mix. I call it a "Hybrid" model, and it is one that particularly suits niche sites, eCommerce, etc. It's a model that relies on the fact that a piece of content does not live on an island. It is related to other pieces of content, which can be grouped and categorized.

This model offers great SEO benefits as well as organizing content in a logical manner to help both visitors and search engines.

Before I tell you the model, let me first distinguish between two types of content that you may have on your site.

The first type of content is the stuff you create for your visitors. It's the content you want your visitors to see and Google to rank highly. We'll call this type of content,

Niche Content. This will include articles, reviews, videos, infographics, etc., that **you create for your targeted audience.**

The second type of content is the stuff that you need to have on the site, but from a financial point of view, you don't really care whether visitors find it. This type of content does not fit into logical groups. Typical examples would be a Privacy page and Terms of Service. I'd also add the "contact" page to this group. I call this type of content my "legal pages."

For the Hybrid model, the rule is to **Use Posts for "Niche Content" and Pages for "Legal Pages."**

The Homepage and About Us are actually the odd pages out, as we obviously want our visitors to see them, yet they don't have any features that would require a WordPress "post." They are not part of a group, are date-independent, and we don't need them in the RSS feed. Therefore, these pages are created using a WordPress Page.

Here is a diagram of the model:

WordPress "Hybrid"

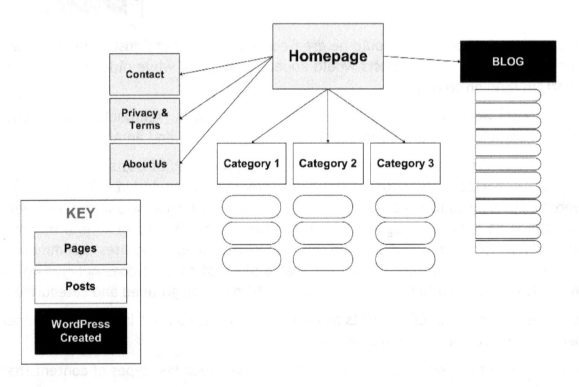

WordPress Pages have been used for Contact, Privacy, Terms, About Us & the Homepage.

The homepage has been created as a static page, which we will look at later in the book.

The site has a number of categories, with posts grouped into those categories. There is also a separate blog for announcements or any other type of short communication you want to put together.

An example of a site that uses this model could be a niche site about Amateur Radios. The homepage might be an article explaining a little about the hobby and what makes it interesting. From the Homepage, you'd see links to the different manufacturers of amateur radio, so Kenwood, Icom & Yaesu. Clicking these links would take you to a category page for that manufacturer, listing all posts on the site that are in that category. The Homepage would also have a link to the site's blog, as well as all the "legal pages."

However, WordPress is so flexible that you might want to design your own structure. See the sections later on categories and tags, as these can help you define your site structure to be truly useful to your visitors and loved by search engines.

16. Setting up the Homepage

There are two main ways of setting up a homepage in WordPress. You can create a WordPress page to use as the homepage, or you set up your homepage to display the latest WordPress posts.

You make that decision in the **Settings -> Reading** options.

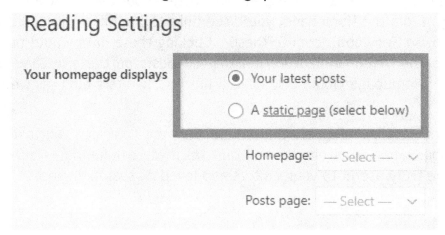

Essentially, using a WordPress page (the static page option in the screenshot) for your homepage means you can have a more static front page, i.e., one that doesn't change too much.

If you choose to go with the latest posts option for your homepage (as is typical for blogs), then it will always be changing, showing your very latest post at the top of it.

For most themes, if you choose a static page for your homepage, you simply select the page that you want to use for your homepage, and you are done. That WordPress page will be displayed as your homepage content.

However, not all WordPress themes are the same.

WordPress themes have evolved, and one of my favorite features of the Genesis theme is the way it handles the homepage. The Genesis framework allows us to create a homepage using widgets.

The Genesis child themes do differ in the number and location of widgetized areas on the homepage, so you would need to check them out before buying one.

For example, the Genesis Lifestyle theme gives you three widgetized areas in addition to the usual header, sidebars, and footers. You have Home, Home left and Home right, and these are positioned directly where the main content of the homepage will go.

Here are those three widget areas:

Those three widget areas can contain posts, pages, or just about anything else.

You can see this theme in action on the Lifestyle demo theme site:

https://demo.studiopress.com/lifestyle/

By contrast, the Genesis Balance theme has two homepage widget areas called **Home Featured Left** and **Home Featured Right**.

Under the **home featured left** and **home featured right** areas of the homepage, the normal WordPress loop is used to show the latest posts in reverse chronological order.

I love the Genesis child themes because they give me so much scope for designing a homepage the way I want it to appear. The idea of using widgets for the homepage, wherever it came from, is pure genius.

Check out all of the Genesis themes here:

https://ezseonews.com/genesis

17. Site-Wide Considerations

There are a couple of things that should be implemented on a site-wide scale.

17.1. "Nofollow" Links

This is a concern for all posts and pages on your entire site.

The nofollow tag can be added to any link to stop the search engines from following it.

Here is an example link with the nofollow attribute assigned to it:

<a href="http://google.com" **rel="nofollow"**>Google</a>

It's a good idea to nofollow links on your site that you don't want to waste link juice on. These include the legal pages (contact, privacy, etc.). We've already seen this earlier in the book when we set up the legal menu to automatically nofollow the links.

I'd also recommend you nofollow *all* affiliate links.

When you are writing content that links to another authority website, do NOT add nofollow. We want Google to know we endorse these other credible sites by leaving the nofollow off the link.

These guidelines go for all pages on your site and not just the homepage.

17.2. Getting Social on Your Site

It is a good idea to include ways for your visitors to follow you and share your content with their followers.

We mentioned a plugin earlier called "Social Media Flying Icons." There are plenty of plugins to choose from, and it will depend on personal choice. My advice, though, is to find one you like and use it. Give your visitors a way to share your content with their audience and to follow you on your social channels.

Google does pay attention to social shares.

18. SEO When Writing Content

In this section, I just want to highlight a few points about writing content and SEO, plus mention the specific features you can use to help with the Search Engine Optimisation on your WordPress pages and WordPress posts.

With any type of content, posts, or pages, it is important to follow a few general rules to ensure you do not fall foul of Google's Panda or Penguin algorithm. In the old days of SEO (pre-2011), webmasters tried to rank specifically for a keyword phrase or two and would insert the exact phrase in several places like the title, filename, H1 header, opening paragraph, closing paragraph, ALT tags, and also worked into various other paragraphs within the article body too. Today that is just asking for trouble. The era of targeting specific words and phrases is just about over.

The best approach to writing good quality content is to write for your visitor and not the search engines. If you write naturally and with a sound knowledge of the topic, you will automatically include relevant words and phrases into your content anyway, which will help it rank for a whole host of search phrases. By all means, include a specific phrase somewhere, such as the title or H1 header, but don't, whatever you do, start stuffing the same phrase in as many places as possible. Google is clever enough now to know what the page is about, even without strategic keyword placements by the webmaster. Concentrate on providing great quality content that will please your visitors, and that Google will want to rank highly because it deserves to.

With that in mind, create a compelling headline for your post, and don't try to stuff it with individual keywords or keyword phrases either. Just aim to create quality content and forget about trying to optimize it for any specific words or phrases.

Tip: If you read your content out loud, and it sounds unnatural because of keywords that have been forced into the text, then it's not great content.

Another thing to think about is the slug of your post or page. The slug is the filename, and it is automatically generated by WordPress when you publish content. WordPress takes your content's title, replaces spaces with dashes, removes any non-alphanumeric characters, and uses that (see below):

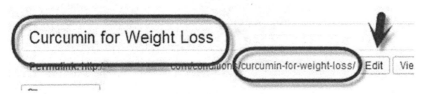

In the screenshot above, the title of the article is **curcumin for weight loss.** The slug that WordPress created is **curcumin-for-weight-loss.**

You can change the slug if you want to; perhaps if there's a better way of naming it, or maybe the title of your article is long (it's a good idea to keep your URLs short). To edit the slug, click the **Edit** button next to the permalink URL at the top of your post/page, and then modify it to what you want. Finally, make sure you Publish/Update your page to save the changes.

18.1. SEO for WordPress Pages

The first thing I should mention about WordPress pages is that they can have comments, though it is disabled by default. This wasn't always the case. I guess WordPress added this feature for sites that are page-based rather than post-based.

You can find the "switch" in the document properties for the page:

If you only use pages for the "legal pages" on your site, then it's unlikely you'll want to enable that option. You don't want people commenting on your privacy policy or contact pages! However, if you do have a page where you would like to enable comments, this is where you do it on a page-by-page basis.

A lot of the SEO we can control on pages (and posts) is supplied to us by the Yoast SEO plugin we saw earlier:

It's identical to the Yoast SEO addition on the edit posts screen we saw earlier. Of particular interest is the **Advanced** tab. I won't go into these settings as we looked at them earlier in the book when setting legal pages to follow, noindex, noarchive.

OK, that's the Yoast SEO settings for WordPress pages. Let's now look at SEO on WordPress posts.

18.2. SEO for WordPress Posts

WordPress posts have a few more SEO options than WordPress pages. We still have the Yoast SEO plugin options that we saw in the previous section on **WordPress Pages**, and they are used in the same way. If you need to noindex, follow a post (as we will do later when we look at setting up category pages), then you do it using the **Advanced** tab of that plugin's options.

Also, you will notice that if you go to **Posts -> All Posts**, in the WordPress Dashboard, there are a few extra columns tacked on to the end of the table:

If you don't see these columns, they are probably turned off in the Yoast SEO settings.

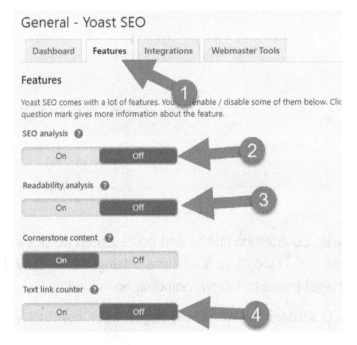

I would suggest you switch these off anyway, at least the first two, which are part of the keyword optimization features in the plugin. Too much optimization for a specific keyword can cause you problems in Google, so turning these off helps you to avoid over-optimization penalties.

18.2.1. Post Categories & Tags

Both categories and tags are ways to categorize your posts.

All posts MUST be assigned to a category, but tags are optional. Categories are, therefore, more important than tags.

While WordPress allows you to put a post into several categories, I highly recommend that a post is only assigned to ONE category. If you think a post can fit equally into two or more categories, I would suggest you are using the wrong categories.

Think of categories as the main way to organize your posts. Think of tags as an additional organizational tool that can be called upon if needed.

Let's consider a website about vacuum cleaners. What would your main categories?

If you had a bunch of vacuum cleaner reviews, how would you want them organized?

What about articles on how to repair different types of vacuum cleaners?

Possibly more importantly, how would your website visitors expect them to be organized? I like to think about what my visitors would want to search for at the site and use that as a starting point.

Here are a few things I believe visitors will search for:

1. Dyson
2. Handheld
3. Dyson Ball
4. Eureka
5. Bagless
6. Cordless
7. Hoover
8. Upright
9. Canister
10. Miele
11. HEPA filter

Which of these should be categories?

If you used all of them as categories, what category would you assign an article about a handheld Dyson vacuum? Dyson, or Handheld?

Clearly, we need to think about this.

Remember, I recommend a post is only assigned to one category. This gives your site a better, clearer structure and will help with SEO. Forcing yourself to think of one category per post can actually help you find the best categories for your site.

Of those ideas listed above, which ones would make the most sense if a vacuum could only be in one category?

How about "bagless"?

Nope. A vacuum could be bagless, upright, and a Dyson.

The obvious categories from that list would be the ones where a vacuum could only fit into one - the brand names. My categories would, therefore, be:

1. Dyson
2. Eureka
3. Hoover
4. Miele

A Dyson DC25 vacuum cleaner review could only go into one category – the Dyson category.

So, what about the other terms:

- Handheld
- Dyson Ball
- Bagless
- Cordless
- Upright
- Canister
- HEPA filter

A vacuum could be cordless, bagless, and contain a HEPA filter! That's a clear indication that these features are not suited as categories. However, they are perfect as tags!

For example, my review of the Dyson DC25 vacuum would be in the category Dyson but could be tagged with ball, HEPA, bagless & upright.

The beauty of using tags is that for every tag you use, WordPress will create a page just for that tag.

The tag page will list ALL posts that have been assigned that tag.

In the example above, WordPress would create FOUR tag pages. One for "ball," one for "HEPA," one for "Bagless," and one for "Upright."

The "HEPA" tag page will list all vacuums on the site that have been tagged with HEPA – it helps visitors find more HEPA vacuums if that is what they are interested in.

Using brand names for categories and features as tags, a visitor can come to the site and find just about anything they want. If they know they want a Dyson, they can go to the Dyson category page and see a list of all Dyson vacuums. If they know they want a handheld vacuum, then they can go to the handheld tag page and see all handheld vacuums, no matter what brand they are.

Tags help search engines too. They provide additional information about an article, helping search engines understand what the content is about.

There is no doubt that tags are powerful. However, with that power comes some responsibility. If you abuse tags, your site will become spammy, and you'll struggle to get any traction in the search engines.

I have seen sites where posts have been tagged with 10, 20, 50, and even several hundred tags. Don't believe me? See this screenshot showing the tags for a post on one website I came across:

You don't need to be able to read the words in that screenshot to get the point. I've had to reduce the size of the screenshot to get all the tags into view. There are over 160 tags for that single post. I happen to know that Google penalized that site.

Every tag on that list will have its own tag page. Many of the tags were only used once on the entire site, so there were 100+ tag pages with just a single post listed as using that tag.

To think about this in another way, if a post lists 160 tags, and this is the only post on the website, then the site will contain over 160 pages. It'll contain one post, 160 tag pages, which are all nearly identical (as they all just list the same post), and a few other pages that WordPress creates for us, which will actually be almost identical to the 160 tag pages.

The way the webmaster used tags in this example is clearly spam, and search engines hate spam. Please, use tags responsibly!

Let's look at one more example.

Think of a recipe website about puddings, desserts, cakes, and so on.

You might have main categories like:

5. Ice cream

6. Cakes

7. Muffins

8. Mousse

9. Cookies

These are the obvious categories since a dessert will only be able to fit into one of the categories. To further classify the recipes on the site, we'd use tags that would add a little more detail about each post.

What type of tags would you use?

Are you stuck for ideas? Think of the "features" of the desserts.

Tags usually choose themselves as you add more content to a website. For example, you might find that a lot of recipes use chocolate, or walnuts, or vanilla, or frosting (you get the idea). These would make perfect tags because a visitor with a hankering for chocolate could visit the chocolate tag page and see a list of all ice cream, cakes, muffins, mousse, and cookies that include chocolate.

Do you see how the tags help with additional layers of categorization? The tag pages become useful pages for visitors.

This is the mindset you are looking to develop as you utilize tags for your own website.

A Few Guidelines for Using Tags

1. Keep a list of tags you use on your site, and make sure you spell them correctly when you reuse them. Remember, if you misspell a tag, another tag page will be created for the misspelled version.

2. Don't create tags that will only apply to one post. Remember, tags are there to help classify your content into groups. Most tags will be used several times on a site, and their use will increase as you add more content. I'd recommend that you only use a tag if it will be used on three or more posts.

3. Only pick a small number of relevant tags per post. I'd recommend somewhere between three and six tags per post, but if some need more, then that's fine. If some need less, that's OK too. This is just a general rule of thumb.

4. NEVER use a tag that is also a category.

Parent Categories & Hierarchy

Categories can be hierarchical. In other words, you can have categories within categories.

An example might be a website about car maintenance. I might have a category called Toyota, but then want sub-categories called Yaris, Auris, Prius, and Land Cruiser for the different maintenance articles on each type of car.

Therefore, the parent category would be Toyota, and the child categories would be Yaris, Auris, Prius, Land Cruiser, etc.

To achieve this, I'd create the Toyota category first, then select it as the parent category when I created the subcategories.

In the list of categories, you can spot parent/child relationships because the parent category is listed first, with the child categories indented below:

Here is a category widget for a site using the structure above:

Categories

Toyota
  Auris
  Land Cruiser
  Prius
  Yaris

You can see how it's possible to preserve the hierarchy in the widget.

Since we installed Yoast SEO as an essential plugin, we now have some extra control over our categories.

Click the **Edit** link underneath one of your categories. The first influence of Yoast SEO is the description editor:

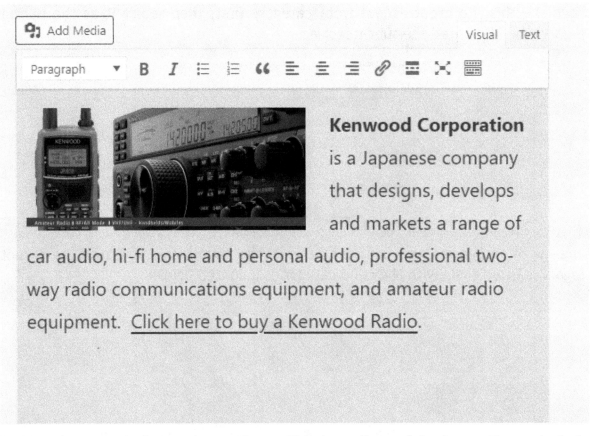

You now have some formatting options. This is really useful when a theme includes the description at the top of a category page. The Twenty Twenty-One theme does this. Here is that Kenwood Category page:

You can see the category description, with formatting and an image, is included at the top of the category page. All posts in the Kenwood category would be listed below.

But there is more. Scroll to the bottom of the edit category screen, and you'll see the Yoast SEO settings:

I have collapsed all of the "tabs" to make the screenshot smaller. But each of those arrows on the right can open up those sections.

The Google preview tab will show you what the category page will look like if listed on Google.

That screenshot shows the preview for **Mobile Results**, so check out what the category page listing would look like on a desktop computer. The radio selector is right above the preview.

That is your search engine listing, more or less. You can see that there is no meta description for that category page, but you can edit aspects of this listing underneath:

As you update these fields, you can watch how your listing appearance will change.

The **Advanced** "tab" will allow you to override the Yoast SEO plugin defaults for this category by choosing whether you want the category page to appear in the search results. Default is yes (that is how we set it up), but you can exclude the category page from the search results by overriding the default setting:

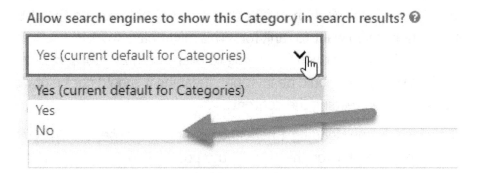

We won't be covering **Canonical URLs** in this book, but you can find out more if you want by clicking the little help button next to that entry.

The social tab allows you to specify title, description, and images that are used when your category page is shared on Facebook or Twitter.

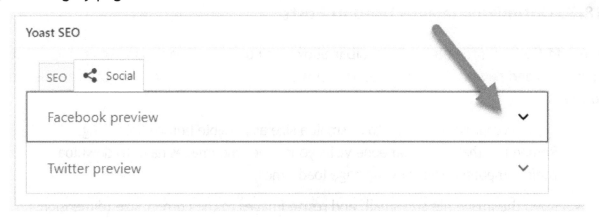

18.2.2. Post Formatting

With formatting comes great responsibility.

With formatting options, like bold, underline & italics, only use them where you would if search engines did not exist. What I mean by that is do not be tempted to put bold or italics on the words and phrases you want to rank for. This might have worked a few years ago, but today it's a signal to Google that you are trying to over-optimize your page for those words and phrases. SEO on your page should be invisible, meaning it should not be obvious what you are trying to rank for when reading the content.

For headers, only include one **Heading 1** headline per page (this uses the H1 HTML tag). Your template is likely to use an H1 for the title of the post, so you shouldn't add a second H1 header. Use headlines in hierarchies, with an H2 being the start of a new section and H3 as subsections of the H2. If you then start a new section, use another H2.

Again, as with all areas of your content, do not stuff keyword phrases into headlines because they'll do you NO favors.

18.3. Optimizing Images Used in Posts

The **Add Media** button above the toolbar allows you to insert images and other media into your posts and pages. For images used in posts, I would recommend you optimize them as follows:

- Try to compress the image to as small a size as possible before uploading. Remember that when someone visits your page, the images have to download to their computers, thus slowing page load times.

- Keep the image file size small, and resize images to the correct size (dimensions) before uploading. For example, if your theme content area is 800 pixels, and you want the image to take up half the width of the content, resize the image so that it is 400 pixels wide.

- Give your image a name that best describes it. Once again, remember not to keyword stuff here, and don't use words and phrases that are irrelevant to the image.

- Use ALT tags for all your images, and I say again, don't keyword stuff. Describe the image appropriately so blind or partially sighted users can understand your content.

- Consider using the Smush Image Compressions and Optimization plugin to automatically optimize images as you upload them to your website. It will also optimize images already in your media library. This optimization will make your images smaller without losing quality. Search for "smush" in the **Add New** plugins screen, and look for this one:

Install and activate the Smush Image Compression and Optimization plugin.

Once activated, you can find the Smush settings in the sidebar menu.

If you visit the Smush dashboard, you'll be taken through a quick setup which will do the hard work of configuration for you.

The free version does have limitations, but it may be all you need.

As the images are processed, the **Stats** panel will be visible in the dashboard:

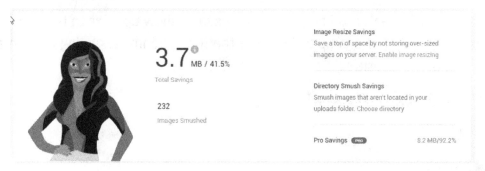

The plugin has a cool feature. It will automatically optimize your images as you upload them. Just make sure that option is selected (it is by default):

The free version of this plugin is enough for most people. However, power users may appreciate the paid features. E.g., The paid version will compress your images up to twice as much as the free version.

18.4. Internal Linking Between Posts

The YARPP plugin we mentioned in the plugins section of this book will create related posts sections on each of your posts if you want them there. That helps to interlink your related content and spread link juice around your site. One of the more powerful on-page techniques is to link words and phrases in one post to another related post, though you shouldn't do this just for the sake of internal linking.

Let me give you an example of how this is used for maximum SEO benefit.

Suppose you had an article called **World's Best Hot Dog Recipe**. In that article, you mention a special tomato sauce that you make for your hot dogs. You have the tomato sauce recipe on your site. It makes sense to link to that tomato sauce recipe from the hot dog recipe article using an "internal link" (i.e., one that goes from one page of your site to another).

Internal linking like this is natural, helps visitors, and is a powerful SEO tool to help our pages rank better.

I experimented with internal linking on one of my sites. I described the experiment and results here:

https://ezseonews.com/backlinks/internal-linking-seo/

18.5. Featured Images for Posts

Posts can be assigned a featured image, which is used to show up next to the post wherever it is listed on your site. For example, here are the featured images being used in a recent posts list on one of my websites:

WordPress.com vs WordPress.org

17/2/2021 - No Comments

The results of our WordPress.com vs WordPress.org guide may surprise you. The pros and cons of WordPress free and for-profit versions help new users make easy decisions.

Read More »

Why is WordPress Free? What Are the Hidden Costs?

12/2/2021 - No Comments

So, why is WordPress free, and what are the hidden costs of this world-renowned open source software? This article answers all, and goes head to head with WordPress.ORG and WordPress.COM.

Read More »

You add featured images to a post directly in the edit post screen (document properties):

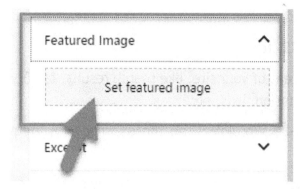

Whether you use them or not depends on how you want your site to look. I think they help break up blocks of text on a web page, therefore helping the visitor to navigate to stuff easier.

If you do use them, make sure you follow the image optimization tips above for these as well. Remember, if you have a list of, say, 20 posts on a category page with 20 featured images, they are going to slow the page load time considerably. Optimizing these images as best you can, both in size (KB) and dimensions (pixels), will help to improve page load speeds.

18.6. Post Excerpts

Excerpts are short summaries of your post. Think of them in the same way as you think of a Meta Description. It should be something short and enticing to the visitor. You can add excerpts in the edit post screen.

Remember, these extracts will be displayed on various areas of your website, serving as descriptions for the posts. Here is the excerpt being used on my site in a recent posts list:

Moving a Site from WordPress.com to WordPress.Org
- So you started your free Wordpress.com website, but now need more power and fewer restrictions. Moving your Wordpress.com site to a Wordpress.org hosted site is easy. This tutorial explains the process.

Excerpts have two main purposes:

1. To add a description to the posts in your RSS feeds.

2. To supply summaries to posts in various areas of your site, like search results, tag & category pages, author pages, meta description, lists, etc.

NOTE: Using the Yoast SEO plugin, you can make WordPress use the excerpt as a meta description.

A good reason to use excerpts is that they provide complete descriptions for any post. If you don't have excerpts written for a post, then WordPress will create a description based on the content of your page, and that will usually stop mid-word or mid-sentence.

I, therefore, recommend writing an excerpt for *all* posts on your site.

18.7. Allow Comments & Trackbacks on Posts?

You can enable or disable comments and trackbacks on posts if you want to, either globally or on a post-by-post basis. I recommend you keep comments enabled on all posts because social interaction is an important aspect of our SEO efforts.

Trackbacks are a little more difficult to give a hard and fast rule about. Essentially, a trackback is like a comment sent to your site from another site when that other site links to yours. While it is nice to know who is linking to us, this feature has been heavily abused by spammers. This means that 99% of the time, a trackback is bogus, and no link exists. The reason the spammers do this is to try to get you to approve their trackback, which then goes live on your site with a link back to theirs. I tend to turn trackbacks off on all posts by default because spammers were taking up too much of my time, constantly checking to see if a site had linked to mine or not. Don't forget that you can choose whether to enable or disable this globally or on a post-by-post basis.

18.8. Scheduling Posts

There may be times when you want to schedule posts into the future. For example, if I am adding 10-20 posts to my site (let's say I just got a bunch of content from my ghostwriter), I would schedule those posts to be released over 2-3 weeks. Doing this encourages the search engine spiders to come back more regularly. It can also encourage visitors to return more often when they see that fresh content is being added frequently.

To schedule posts, look for the "Status & Visibility" section of the Document properties for the post. You'll see an item that is set to **Immediately** by default. Immediately is a hyperlink, so to schedule a post, click it:

You'll get a calendar to select the date and time you want the post to be published.

When that date and time arrives, WordPress automatically publishes the article for you. You do not have to login or do anything else once this is set up.

If you want to bulk schedule posts for a site, consider using the Editorial Calendar plugin.

This gives you a drag-and-drop calendar interface for scheduling your posts.

18.9. A Checklist for Good SEO Content

Writing good SEO content is a huge topic. I've written an entire book and video course on the subject. However, I wanted to include a quick summary of the main points you should check off as you publish content on your site.

18.9.1. Titles

1. Titles are one of the most important areas of a web page, both in terms of SEO and getting click-throughs from the search engines. The title needs to appeal to the searcher.

2. Titles are automatically converted into URLs by WordPress. A setting in the Yoast SEO plugin can automatically strip out stop words from the URL. I recommend you use that (see later). Also, consider manually editing the filename to include a different keyword than the title.

3. Include your primary keywords in the title if you can, but don't stuff it. Words that appear at the beginning of the title are given more emphasis by Google, so insert the most important keyword as close to the start of the title as possible.

4. Try to minimize the use of stop words. These are the short, unimportant words that can dilute the importance of keywords. Examples include "the," "it," "of," etc.

5. Limit the title to less than 60 characters in length. A good length to shoot for is 55. Any longer and it will become truncated in the search results. You can use the snippet preview supplied by the Yoast SEO plugin to help check titles.

18.9.2. Headings

1. You can use H1, H2, H3, H4, H5 & H6 headings on a web page.

2. Your web page should contain only one H1 heading. Most WordPress themes automatically use if for the post title, so don't use any more H1 headings in your content.

3. Use H2 and H3 in a hierarchical manner. Split up the article into sections using H2 headers. If a section needs to be further divided into sections, use H3 headers within the H2. I don't recommend you use H4, H5, or H6 headers. WordPress themes often use these in the sidebars, and they are given very little attention by the search engines.

18.9.3. Theme Your Content

This is a huge topic! Please see my other books and courses if you want in-depth help with this. The basics are simple, though.

When you write content, don't focus on one or two keywords. Choose a topic to write about. The topic can be a broad, top-level keyword. Then find out what keywords and phrases SHOULD be included in that topic and try to incorporate as many as possible on your web page.

For example, if I had a health site, I might target the keyword "gestational diabetes." Rather than try to create a page around the term "gestational diabetes," I would find out what other words and phrases are needed to create a compressive, authoritative piece of content. They would include words like:

Blood sugar, blood pressure, hypertension, glucose, pregnancy, baby, birth, pre-eclampsia, insulin, glucose tolerance test, type 2 diabetes, screening, treatment, etc.

When writing the content, your focus should be on all of these words and phrases, not just "gestational diabetes."

18.9.4. Categories & Tags

5. Only ever assign one category to a post. If you think your post can fit into two or more, chances are you have chosen the wrong categories.

6. Use tags sparingly. Remember that WordPress creates a tag page for each one used.

7. Only ever assign a tag to a post if that tag is used (or will be used) for several posts. I would recommend 3 or 4 tags maximum per post, but you can also decide not to use tags if you prefer.

8. Use tags to create related groups within your categories. Categories and tags should work together and complement each other.
   For example, I might have a category called "Type 2 Diabetes" and tags for "symptoms," "treatment," etc.

18.9.5. Images

1. ALT tags help visually impaired visitors to your website. Create good, accurate ALT tags for your images. Do not try to stuff keywords into these tags.

2. Give images a descriptive name that might contain a keyword phrase.

3. Remember that images used in your content may be used if people share your content on social media channels.

4. Try to include an image near the beginning of your web page. Visitors are more likely to see the image and continue reading your content than if they just see a wall of text.

5. Optimize your images before you upload them. If your web page content loads inside an 800-pixel wide "text box" and you want the image to take up half of the width, resize the image to 400-pixels wide before uploading.

6. If you have an image compression plugin like Smush, use it.

7. Run your pages through GTMetrix.com to check if any images are causing page loading delays.

18.9.6. Excerpts

1. Always include a descriptive excerpt with your posts. These can be used for post descriptions on your site, but also the meta description of the web page. Google may also use it as the description of your post in the search results.

2. The except should be unique from the title and complement it.

3. Imagine your excerpt appearing as your post description in Google. Try to create excerpts that entice the click from searchers.

18.9.7. Linking to Other Content

- The internet was built on links. Don't be afraid to link out to web pages on authority websites using dofollow links.

- If you link to a page that you don't "trust," use the nofollow tag.

- Link to your "legal pages" using nofollow.

- Link to other pages on your site where appropriate. Check out how Wikipedia links to related content on Wikipedia from every page on their site. I don't recommend you internally link as much as Wikipedia, but certainly, if you have relevant content to refer to in an article, link to it. This type of internal link is the only acceptable way to get keyword-rich anchor text into a link to your content. The C.I. Backlinks plugin mentioned on the resources page for this book is a great way of automating this naturally.

- Use YARPP or a similar plugin to provide relevant links to related content.

19. Setting up Category Pages

Categories are used to classify posts. When you create a new post, you file it away in a particular category. As your site grows, categories will start to fill up with more and more relevant, related content.

For every category you create, WordPress will create a category page. This will list all of the posts within that category.

This helps visitors and search engines alike.

When you set up a category on your site, I highly recommend you give your new category a description.

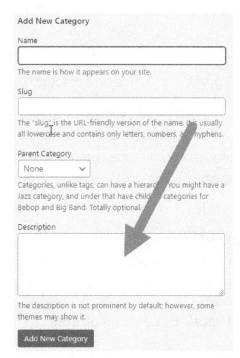

Some themes will use these descriptions in a variety of places, but the most important place is the category page itself as an introduction. If your theme supports this, and I suggest you find one that does, your category pages suddenly become a lot more useful and interesting to visitors and search engines.

That is, as long as it doesn't force full post content on you.

19.1. A Category Page Full Post Content

A typical category page looks something like this, with or without the introduction at the top:

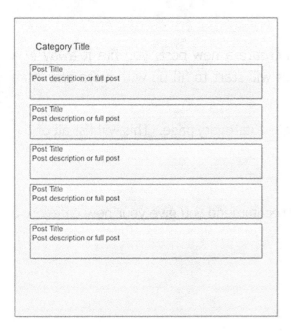

Depending on the theme you are using, those posts may be showing as a title with an excerpt or a title with a full post. The latter would cause huge duplication problems since these category pages would contain the complete text of all posts within the category.

You should choose a theme that allows you to use post excerpts on category (and tag) pages. If you don't have a choice and the theme displays full posts on these pages, then these pages won't serve as useful content. Instead, they'll cause you a nightmare of duplication problems that Google will not be happy about.

There is a solution, though.

If your category page uses the full post text, then you should set the category pages (and probably tag pages) to noindex. This means that search engines will find them and follow the links on these pages but won't index and include them in the search results. Since we only want valuable pages/posts to appear in the search engine, this is what we want.

Thanks to the Yoast SEO plugin, achieving this is easy.

The Yoast SEO plugin allows you to treat categories and tag pages globally or on a page-by-page basis. Therefore, you can globally set all category pages to *noindex*, or you can set just one or two category pages to *noindex*. The same goes for tag pages, posts, pages, etc.

19.1.1. Globally Set All Category Pages to Noindex

To make *all* category page *noindex*, go to the **SEO -> Search Appearance** section and click on the **Taxonomies** tab.

Set the **Show Categories in search results?** option to **No**.

You can do this for tag pages, too, if necessary.

This setting makes these archive page noindex, follow. That means they won't appear in the search engines, but links on the pages will be followed.

Although probably less useful for most websites, you can also set category and tab pages to noindex on a one-by-one basis.

19.1.2. Setting Individual Category Pages to Noindex

To make category pages *noindex, follow* on a page-by-page basis, you need to go to the **Posts -> Categories** section of the Dashboard and click on a category you want to modify.

Note: You need to create the category first and then go in and edit it because these extra options are not found on the main screen from where you create new categories.

When you go into the category edit screen, there are several new options available to you, thanks to Yoast's SEO plugin. These should look very familiar to you:

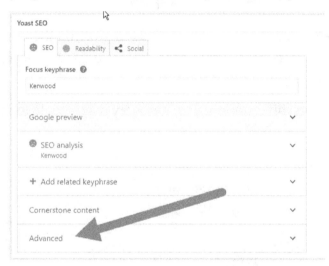

The options in this Yoast SEO box allow us to override any or all of the global category settings. These are the same settings you have for every post and page on your site too!

On the **Advanced** tab, you can choose not to allow the page to appear in the search results. That will mean Google won't index and rank these pages, which is what we want.

19.2. The Ideal Category Page?

A category page becomes useful when it includes:

- An Introduction
- A list of posts in the category, with hyperlinked title to the article and a short description (excerpt).

Our category pages would then look like this:

On this category page, there is a text introduction to the category, followed by post Titles and post Excerpts of all the articles within the category.

The written introduction adds SEO benefits in that this page now has some unique content on it and introduces the posts in the category to both visitors and search engines. This is the type of category (and tag) page that I strive for on all of my websites. Set up this way, you can leave *all* of the category pages as *index, follow*. This is because they are now genuinely useful pages for a visitor.

To get this type of category page, your theme needs to give you the option of using excerpts (instead of full posts) on category and tag pages (or if you can find a plugin that works with your theme to add this feature).

Assuming your theme meets this criterion, your category page should look something like this:

Prebiotics

As we've seen on the homepage of this site, a prebiotic is kind of like a bacterial fertilizer targeting the good bacteria in our guts. In order to be considered a prebiotic, a substance must exhibit three properties:

1. The fibre must be resistant to human digestion. The prebiotic needs to feed the good bacteria, not the human.
2. The fibre needs to be fermentable by the good bacteria in your gut.
3. The fibre should selectively stimulate colonies of good bacteria in your gut.

Prebiotics are found naturally in the plant food that we eat.

Prebiotics Fibre Foods and Supplements

Prebiotic fiber ferments in the small and large intestines. This is a process where they get to release nutrients for your healthy gut flora to feed on.

What are the best Prebiotic Supplements?

Prebiotic supplements are not all the same. The best ones are the full spectrum prebiotics I mention in this

Notice the introduction at the top of the category page, followed by links to the posts in that category, with a short excerpt being used as the description.

19.3. Formatting the introduction

When you create a category, the description box is a plain text editor, meaning you cannot format your descriptions.

There is a way, though, and it is already installed in your Dashboard. It's the Yoast SEO plugin to the rescue again.

Go back to the **Posts** -> **Categories** screen, and click on the category you want to edit.

Thanks to the Yoast SEO plugin (make sure it is installed and activated), you know have a WYSIWYG editor for your descriptions:

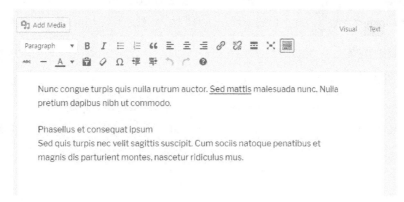

To access this WYSIWYG editor for descriptions (and tag pages), you need to create the category first, then go in and edit it.

Using this editor, I can format the introduction the way I want:

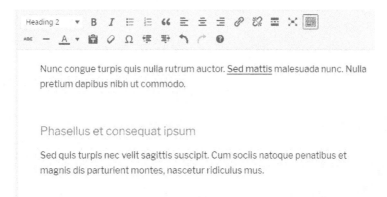

The editor will also allow you to insert images and any other formatting that you normally have available to you when entering posts or pages.

Using this powerful category (and tag) page description editor, it's possible to create great, interesting, and valuable introductions for all category and tag pages.

20. Tag Pages

We've just seen how to create valuable category pages that can (and deserve to) rank well in the search engines. Tag pages can rank remarkably well because they tend to have a lot of internal links pointing at them (from all posts that use that tag). With the added introduction, they become really valuable pages. For this reason, I like to have tag pages set up in the same way we did for category pages.

The process is identical to category pages.

If you go and edit an existing tag (**Posts -> Tags**), you'll get the same Yoast SEO settings we saw with the category pages, allowing you to create a custom Title and Description as well as being able to *noindex* a tag page and exclude it from the sitemap if you need to.

To be useful, the theme's tag page needs to give you the option of using excerpts (instead of full posts) on tag pages.

Just follow the same advice for tags as we discussed for category pages. If tag pages don't allow excerpts, then noindex them (or see if you can find a plugin that can add this feature to work with your theme).

21. Yoast SEO Plugin Setup

Yoast's SEO plugin provides a massive amount of SEO control over your WordPress site. When you install it, you'll find SEO options popping up in several areas of your Dashboard (as we've already seen). These areas can be divided into two main parts; those that control global settings and those that override global settings on a one-by-one basis.

We've already seen how the plugin can be used to change the SEO settings on a post-by-post, page-by-page, or archive-by-archive (category & tag pages), so let's focus now on the global settings.

21.1. Dashboard Settings

The **Global** settings are found in the SEO menu of the WP Dashboard:

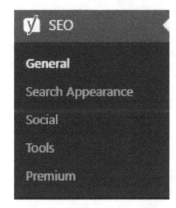

Think of the global settings as the **default settings** for every post and page on your site.

e.g., Making the category pages noindex in these global settings will mean all category pages on the site will be set to noindex by default. As you have seen, these default settings can be overridden on a category-by-category basis.

21.1.1. General

OK, let's look at these "Global Settings."

Click on **SEO** -> **General**.

Across the top, you'll see three tabs – Dashboard, Features, and Webmaster Tools.

You are currently on the **Dashboard** tab. This is used to notify you of problems or other notifications. For example, there is a notification that offers to help you configure the plugin:

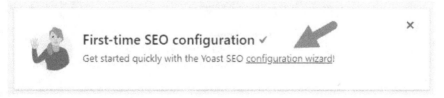

We are going to go through the configuration wizard so you can see what it covers. This is not essential as we will go through all of the settings manually. Therefore, you can skip this if you want.

OK, let's start. Click on the "configuration wizard" link to start.

You'll be taken to the "environment" screen:

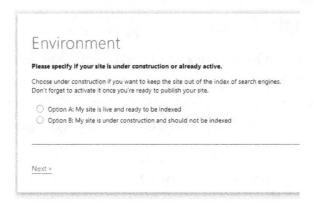

Select the option that applies and click **Next**. You'll be asked what type of site you are setting up:

Select the most appropriate option, and click **next**.

Note that you can change these settings later, so don't worry too much if you are unsure of any settings.

The next screen is asking whether you are an organization or a person:

If you select **Person**, then it will ask you for the name of the person, drawing the options available from the user profiles in your Dashboard.

If you choose **Organisation**, it will ask for the name and a company logo. You'll also have options for adding all of your social media channels that you want to be included in the metadata for the site.

Once done, click **Next** to be taken to the **Search Engine Visibility** screen. This sets the default index/noindex values for posts and pages. Setting an option to **no** means it will be tagged noindex.

Make your choices and click **Next** to go to the **Multiple Authors** screen. If there is only one author, the author's archive page feature will be deactivated to prevent duplicate content issues. If you have more than one author, author archives are enabled.

Clicking Next continues the setup process. On the next screen, you'll be asked to choose a title separator character:

When someone visits your website, WordPress creates the page on-the-fly. It builds the title of the page according to the settings you have in the SEO plugin. By default, the title may include the post title and site name. What you are choosing in these settings is the character that would appear between post title and site name in the title. Make your choice and click **Next**.

That completes the wizard.

Scroll to the bottom and click **Next**.

Scroll to the bottom and click **Close**.

We are now back where we started in the Dashboard settings. Some of the settings in the plugin will have been updated, depending on your choices, but we can go in and manually change anything.

Let's work our way through the settings. We've already mentioned the **Dashboard** tab, so click on the **Features** tab.

This allows you to switch the features of the plugin on or off. We saw this earlier when I suggested you might want to switch off the three columns in the "All Posts" view.

The options you can turn on/off are as follows:

- SEO Analysis – analyses your text and makes suggestions. I turn this off.

- Readability Analysis – How readable is your content? This option offers suggestions to improve structure and style. I turn this off.

- Cornerstone content – Mark and filter content as "cornerstone." I turn this off.

- Text Link Counter – Counts links on your pages. I turn this off.

- XML Sitemaps – Enables an XML sitemap on your site. This should be ON.

- Ryte Integration – checks the indexability of your site. I turn this off.

- Admin Bar menu – Adds a menu to the **admin bar** (visible when visiting your site and logged in), which adds useful links to tools.

- Security: no advanced settings for authors – removes privileges from the author's role. I don't have multiple authors, so this is irrelevant.

I have included my settings for these features, but you may want to use some that I don't. It all depends on how you work. If you do make changes, be sure to **Save Changes**.

On the **Webmaster Tools** tab, you can integrate your site with popular services, like Google Search Console. Each integration option has a link to help you with the integration.

21.1.2. Search Appearance

Click on the **Search Appearance** menu in the sidebar. These options define how the various web pages on your site appear in the search engines.

This screen has several tabs:

- General – settings for the homepage.

- Content Types – settings for posts and pages.

- Media – settings for media & attachment pages.

- Taxonomies – settings for category pages, tag pages & post formats

- Archives – settings for author archives, date archives, search pages, and 404 pages.

- Breadcrumbs – allows you to enable breadcrumb navigation on your site. This does require some coding, so don't think it is a simple on/off switch.

- RSS – settings for your RSS feeds.

Let's look briefly at these tabs.

The **General** tab refers to your homepage.

You can set a separator that might be used in your page title, e.g., between the page title and the site name.

You have options to set the SEO title and meta description for the homepage. These both allow you to use variables for quickly inserting information into the fields.

In the screenshot above, the SEO title created when the homepage is rendered will be:

The site's title, followed by the separator we defined a moment ago, followed by the site's tagline. For the homepage, variables are less useful, but for posts and pages, they become really important.

You'll also have some options on this screen to add or edit the knowledge graph and schema details of the page. What you see depends on whether you chose a person or an organization for your site. This metadata is used by Google to help create rich snippets in the search results.

Over on the **Content Types** tab, you have options for posts and pages. These include the same SEO Title and meta description we just saw. In this case, variables are much more useful.

Since every post is different, we need the post title to update depending on which post is viewed in the web browser. The above variable makes this possible. When a post is viewed in a browser, the post's title will be made up of:

- The title of the post as shown on the edit post screen.

- The separator we chose for the site on the General tab.

- The website's title.

Using variables makes the creation of the SEO title dynamic, changing for every post viewed.

You also get an option of whether or not to show these pages in the search results. Choosing no will set the default to noindex for that content type.

You get the option to hide the date in any Google preview.

The other interesting option is the **Yoast SEO Meta Box**. This will show or hide the Yoast SEO settings on the post/page edit screens. As these are useful, you should leave them as **Show**.

The options you get for **Taxonomies** and **Archives** are very similar. Just work your way through these settings and save when done.

The **RSS** options allow you to inject content before and after each entry in the feed.

RSS feed settings ❓

Content to put before each post in the feed	
Content to put after each post in the feed	The post %%POSTLINK%% appeared first on %%BLOGLINK%%.

Again, you have variables to help you add relevant content:

Available variables ❓

Variable	Description
%%AUTHORLINK%%	A link to the archive for the post author, with the authors name as anchor text.
%%POSTLINK%%	A link to the post, with the title as anchor text.
%%BLOGLINK%%	A link to your site, with your site's name as anchor text.
%%BLOGDESCLINK%%	A link to your site, with your site's name and description as anchor text.

21.1.3. Social

Click on the **Social** link in the SEO menu. The social settings are spread over several tabs:

What you see on your **Accounts** tab depends on whether your metadata is set up for a person or organization. If you have chosen a **person**, then this tab is disabled. If you have chosen an organization, then you are given options for connecting to your social media channels.

If you went through the configuration wizard, you might already have these populated. However, this screen allows you to come in and manually update/edit/add social URLs.

Once you are done, click on the **Facebook** tab.

Facebook's Open Graph is used by a lot of search engines and social websites to tell them information about your site and about the pages they are visiting.

On the Facebook tab, enable **Add Open Graph Data**. Note that several plugins offer to add this data to your pages. Only enable it in one plugin (this SEO plugin).

With this checked, the plugin will add Facebook Open Graph Meta Tags to your pages:

```
https://yoast.com/wordpress/plugins/seo/ -->
<meta name="description" content="Krill Oil v Fish Oil - The Story There
so much is being written about krill oil and fish oil; both are excellen'
fa"/>
<meta name="robots" content="noindex,follow,noodp"/>
<link rel="canonical" href="http://fishyfats.com/" />
<meta property="og:locale" content="en_US" />
<meta property="og:type" content="website" />
<meta property="og:title" content="Krill Oil v Fish Oil - The Story | Fi:
<meta property="og:description" content="Krill Oil v Fish Oil - The Story
reason why so much is being written about krill oil and fish oil; both a
Omega-3 fa" />
<meta property="og:url" content="http://fishyfats.com/" />
<meta property="og:site_name" content="Fishy Fats" />
<meta property="og:image" content="http://fishyfats.com/wp-content/uploa(
3.jpg" />
<meta name="twitter:card" content="summary" />
<meta name="twitter:description" content="Krill Oil v Fish Oil - The Stor
reason why so much is being written about krill oil and fish oil; both a
Omega-3 fa" />
```

You now have an option to add default title, description, and image values used in the Open Graph meta tags on the front page of your site.

You also have default settings where you can do the same for posts and pages.

OK, that's all we are doing on the Facebook tab. Let's move over to the **Twitter** tab.

Social - Yoast SEO

| Accounts | Facebook | **Twitter** | Pinterest |

Twitter settings

Twitter uses Open Graph metadata just like Facebook, so be sure to keep the "Add Open Graph meta data" setting on the Facebook tab enabled if you want to optimize your site for Twitter.

Add Twitter card meta data

| Enabled | Disabled |

Enable this feature if you want Twitter to display a preview with images and a text excerpt when a link to your site is shared.

The default card type to use

Summary with large image

Save changes

You can leave these settings on the default. This will add Twitter metadata to your web pages.

```
<meta name="twitter:card" content="summary" />
<meta name="twitter:description" content="Omega-3 fatty acids
required by every cell in your body. This article discusses wh
3." />
<meta name="twitter:title" content="Omega-3 deficiency | Fishy
<meta name="twitter:site" content="@FishyFats" />
<meta name="twitter:image" content="http://fishyfats.com/wp-cc
<meta name="twitter:creator" content="@FishyFats" />
<!-- / Yoast SEO plugin. -->
```

When anyone tweets with a link to your site, the tweet will contain the usual stuff, but Twitter also scrapes the card data.

You can find out more information if you search Google for "Twitter cards."

The final tab is the **Pinterest** options.

This screen lets you confirm your site with Pinterest. Just follow the instruction on this page.

21.1.4. Tools

There are three tools included with this plugin. We won't go into detail other than to summarize what they do.

The import and export tools let you import and export settings from one SEO plugin to another and from one website to another. We won't be looking at them here.

The file editor tool gives you quick access to the robots.txt and .htaccess files. If you don't have a robots.txt file, this tool can help you create one. See earlier for my recommendation that you don't need one.

The bulk editor allows you to save time with multiple title and description changes. Instead of having to go into the edit screen for each post and page, you can use this bulk edit tool. It looks like this:

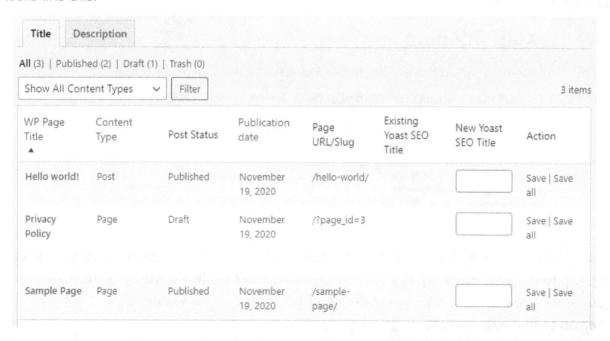

The two tabs across the top give you access to title and description data. The last but one column allows you to quickly type in a new "SEO Title" (and "SEO Description" on the description tab).

21.2. XML Sitemaps

Earlier in the setup of this plugin, we kind of glossed over the XML sitemap other than to say it should be turned on. In this section, I want to go back to the sitemap and look at it in a little more detail.

From the SEO menu, select **General** and then click on the **Features** tab.

Scroll down to the **XML Sitemaps** section and click on the small "question mark" icon:

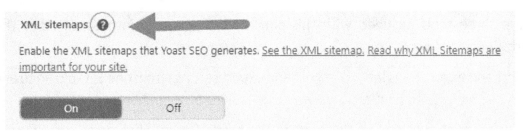

Make sure the sitemap feature is turned on.

You'll see a link to **See the XML Sitemap**. Clicking this opens the sitemap created by the Yoast SEO plugin.

NOTE: This feature won't be available if you have used Local by Flywheel to install WordPress locally on your computer.

XML Sitemap

Generated by YoastSEO, this is an XML Sitemap, meant for consumption by search engines.

You can find more information about XML sitemaps on sitemaps.org.

This XML Sitemap Index file contains 3 sitemaps.

Sitemap	Last Modified
http://ezseonews.com/post-sitemap.xml	2021-02-17 21:35 +00:00
http://ezseonews.com/page-sitemap.xml	2021-02-18 11:33 +00:00
http://ezseonews.com/category-sitemap.xml	2021-02-17 21:35 +00:00

Having an XML sitemap for your site is important. While it's not much use to visitors, it's a big help to search engines, as they use it to find your site's content. With good navigation on your site, a search box, and a well-designed homepage, your visitors should not need a sitemap to find your content!

You can see three sitemaps listed in that screenshot. Yoast SEO creates separate sitemaps for posts, pages, categories, tags, etc. In that list, each of those is a separate sitemap, and you can click the link to see what is contained in each sitemap. For example, my category sitemap looks like this:

You may have noticed that my main sitemap does not include one for tags. That's because I turned that off on this site using the Yoast SEO settings:

This setting will also add noindex to all Tag pages.

If there is a particular post you want to hide on the sitemap but have posts globally enabled on the sitemap, you can go in and edit the post in question and change the Yoast settings on that post only:

21.2.1. Submitting Your Sitemap(s) to Google

Earlier in the book, I recommended you sign up for Google Search Console (GSC). One of the reasons was to submit your sitemap(s) to Google so that your site would be spidered and indexed quicker. By submitting your sitemap to Google, you are telling them directly that these are the important URLs for them to consider.

The first step is to log in to GSC and select the site you are working on. Then, in the side menu, click on **Sitemaps**.

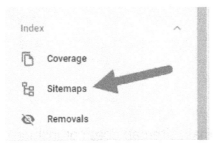

On the right-hand side of the screen, you can **Add a new sitemap:**

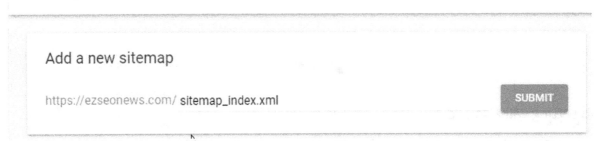

Complete the URL of your sitemap by adding **sitemap_index.xml** and then click on the **Submit** button.

Your newly submitted sitemap will be shown as pending. It usually takes a minute or two for Google to visit the sitemap and report back, so just wait a couple of minutes, and then refresh your browser. You should then see confirmation that Google processed your sitemap. As Google spiders your site, this table will populate to give you more details:

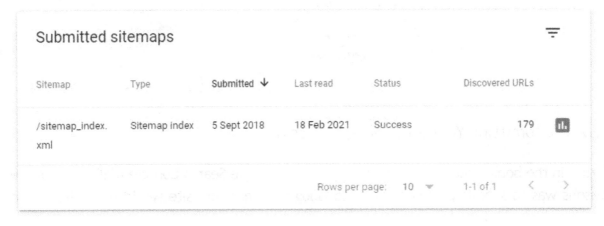

22. Caching Plugin

Page load times are really important in SEO terms. If a page takes a long time to load, a visitor won't wait around. Instead, they'll click the back button and return to Google – something called a "bounce." The bounce rate is something Google takes notice of. If a page has a high bounce rate and that bounce takes place within a few seconds of a user clicking a link in the SERPs, what does that tell Google about the page they tried to visit?

With WordPress, we use caching plugins to speed up the load times of our sites. Caching plugins generally create static HTML versions of our pages on the server, which can be served a lot faster than a WordPress page rendering from scratch. Every time a visitor accesses a page, the cached version is served up quickly.

There are several caching plugins available. Some are paid, others are free. I am going to show a basic setup for W3 Cache, a top-rated free caching plugin. However, if you use a host that uses LiteSpeed servers, I recommend a different caching plugin. The host I use and recommend is based on Litespeed servers, so if you have followed my recommendation, I do recommend you set up the LiteSpeed caching plugin instead of W3 Total Cache. It may already be installed by default.

22.1. Litespeed Cache

This is the plugin I recommend for sites hosted on Litespeed servers.

Before installing, head on over to GTMetrix.com and run a speed test on your site. Here are the results for one of my sites:

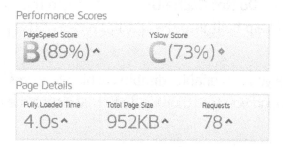

So my test page is taking 4.0 seconds to load, is 952 KB in size, and required 78 requests on the server to fully load. The overall Pagespeed score is B (89%).

So let's install the Litespeed caching plugin and activate it.

Clicking on the Litespeed Cache menu in the left sidebar takes us to the settings. The first thing to do is enable caching, so enable the **Enable LiteSpeed Cache:**

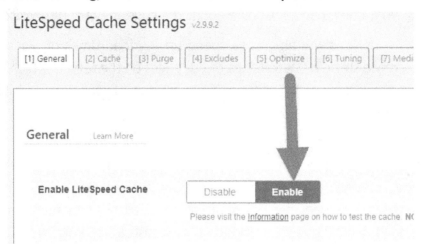

Scroll to the bottom and **Save Changes**.

I am not going to go through all of the settings of this plugin, but I do want to get you started.

On the **Purge** tab, make sure **Purge All On Upgrade** is enabled. This will make sure that you avoid caching problems when any part of WordPress is updated. The **Auto Purge Rules** define which caches are cleared when a post is published or updated. When you think about how WordPress works, when a post is updated, several pages are updated. Therefore, do you want those pages purged when a post is updated? You can check the boxes to ensure they are.

Another useful area of the settings is **Excludes**. You will find some plugins don't work well with caches. This area allows us to exclude certain sections or pages of our site from being cached. You can use string matching when defining areas to not cache. For example, if you run a forum on your site, and all forum posts are within a folder called "forum," you can include "/forum/" in the **Do Not Cache URIs** box to avoid the forum from being cached. There is plenty of help built into the settings pages of this plugin, so make use of it.

The **Optimize** tab is where you can enable/disable caching features. When enabling any of these caches, I do recommend you test thoroughly to make sure the caching is working properly. If you want to know what any of the settings do, please follow the links to help within the plugin settings screen.

Here are the settings that I have turned on in my set up:

- CSS Minify
- CSS Combine
- JS Minify
- JS Combine
- HTML Minify
- Inline CSS Minify
- Inline JS Minify
- Load CSS Asynchronously
- Generate Critical CSS
- Generate Critical CSS in Background
- Inline CSS Async Lib

Make sure you save any changes you make.

Once done, you can re-run the report on GTMetrix.com to see if your measures improved load times. Here's my new report:

So the homepage now takes 2.3 seconds to load, with only 34 requests, compared to 4.0 seconds and 78 requests previously.

You can further fine-tune the caching plugin on the **Tuning** tab.

Do be careful about making changes on that page.

OK, so that is the Litespeed cache which I recommend if your server is a Litespeed server. If you are on any other type of server, I recommend you use W3 Total Cache.

22.2 W3 Total Cache Setup

W3 Total Cache is one of several good WordPress caching plugins.

If you are a WordPress veteran and have always used, and are happy with a different caching plugin, then I suggest you continue to use it.

If you have used W3 Total Cache before and know how to set it up, you can ignore this section.

Setting up W3 Total cache can be a little hit and miss sometimes, with some servers (or scripts on pages) disliking specific things you try to enable. It is, therefore, imperative that you make a backup of your database before you start to set up this plugin. The UpdraftPlus plugin mentioned earlier in the plugins section of this book is ideal for that.

I won't be covering all of the settings of this plugin. I will set you up with a good basic configuration, though, and one which should be compatible with most servers, templates, plugins, and scripts. However, if you find your site has any problem loading, simply reverse the changes you made, or deactivate the plugin altogether.

Before we start, I recommend you head over to GTMetrix.com and measure the speed of your site homepage. Here is mine:

Re-test a total of three times, and take an average of load times.

We'll now set up W3 Total Cache and retest.

I will assume you have already installed and activated the plugin since we covered that earlier.

In your WordPress Dashboard, you have several sub-menus under the **Performance** menu.

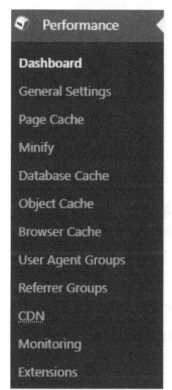

NOTE: Your best option for setting up this plugin would be to ask your web host for their recommended settings. That way, you can be sure you have the best options for your host. However, I will show you my own settings.

General Settings

Click on the **General Settings** menu item.

This is where we can toggle the various caches on or off.

At the top of the page, you have the option of enabling a **Preview Mode**. The preview mode will allow you to open up a preview window to see how the changes you've made are affecting your site before they go live. When you are happy with your settings, you can disable preview mode and save your settings. At that point, they will go live on your site.

If you want to use preview mode, that's fine. I am not going to bother.

Let's go and start enabling caches. Here are the settings.

Page Cache:

1. Enable page cache.

2. Page cache method – Disk enhanced.

Minify:

1. Enable minify.

2. Minify mode set to auto.

3. Minify cache method – Disk.

4. HTML minifier – Default.

5. JS Minifier – JSMin (default).

6. CSS minifier – Default.

Database Cache:

1. Enable database cache.

2. Database Cache Method – Disk

Object Cache:

1. Enable object cache.

2. Object cache method – Disk.

Browser cache:

1. Enable browser cache.

CDN:

Leave disabled for now. This is something you can activate and set up later, but you should contact your host support first, as some hosts, like StableHost, have easy integration with CDN. I use Stablehost and their free CDN, and it made a big difference to the stability and speed of my site.

All other settings on the General Settings menu can be left at their default values.

Make sure you click the **Save Settings & Purge Caches** button before moving on.

Click on the **Page Cache** menu in the sidebar.

22.1.2. Page Cache

General:

These should all be disabled except:

Enable Cache posts page.

Enable Cache feeds.

Cache SSL (HTTPS) requests.

Cache requests only for your domain site address.

Enable Don't cache pages for logged in users.

Leave all other settings in the Page Cache at their default settings.

22.1.3. Minify

General:

1. Enable Rewrite URL structure.

Leave these other settings at their default.

HTML & XML:

1. Enable HTML minify settings.

2. Check Inline CSS minification.

3. Check inline JS minification.

4. Check line break removal.

22.1.4. Browser Cache

General:

1. Enable set last-modified header.

2. Enable set expires header.

3. Enable set cache control header.

4. Enable Entity tag (eTag).

5. Enable W3 Total Cache header.

6. Enable HTTP (gzip compression).

That's it! Your W3 Total Cache is now configured with conservative settings.

Using the Admin bar at the top of your website, purge all caches from the **Performance** menu.

Now go back to GTMetrix.com and check your homepage speed. After the first check, re-test it a second time. The first time will take longer as the page won't be cached yet. The second run will give you a better idea of your true page load time.

As a reminder, here was mine **BEFORE** installing W3 Total Cache:

And here is the same page **AFTER** W3 cache was installed and configured (these are the results on the second run after clearing the cache):

The homepage is now loading nearly two seconds quicker, with far fewer requests on the server. The total page size is down a little too. I'll probably check the images on this page to see if any large ones need to be better optimized. The Smush Image Compressions and Optimization plugin could help with this.

That's it. Your WordPress site is now highly optimized for the search engines and loads quickly. Congratulations!

Where to Go from Here?

We've covered a lot of ground in this book. You are now proficient in the on-site SEO that WordPress requires. There are some resources that you might find interesting and relevant.

All resources mentioned in this book can be found here:

https://ezseonews.com/wpseo

YouTube Channel

Lots of video tutorials on using WordPress.

http://ezseonews.com/yt

O.M.G. Facebook Group

A group I initially created for my course students, but I welcome book readers too! Meet, chat, and discuss with other WordPress users. This is an ad-free zone, so you won't be bombarded with people trying to sell you stuff. You will be asked where you heard about the group when you click to join, so just say you are a reader of the book.

http://ezseonews.com/omg

My Site / Newsletter

Find lots of WordPress tutorials. You can sign up for my newsletter while you are there to get notified of new tutorials, books, courses, etc.

https://ezseonews.com/

There are a few places that I would recommend you visit for more information.

WordPress Tutorials on my Website

https://ezseonews.com/category/wordpress/

My Other Webmaster Books

All my books are available as Kindle books and paperbacks. You can view them all here:

https://amazon.com/author/drandrewwilliams

I'll leave you to explore those if you are interested. You'll find books on various aspects of being a webmaster, such as creating high-quality content, SEO, CSS, etc.

My Video Courses

I have a growing number of video courses hosted on Udemy. You can view a complete list of these at my site:

https://ezseonews.com/udemy

There are courses on the same kinds of topics that my books cover, so SEO, Content Creation, WordPress, Website Analytics, etc.

Google Webmaster Guidelines

https://ezseonews.com/wmg – this is the webmaster's bible of what is acceptable and what is not in the eyes of the world's biggest search engine.

WordPress Glossary

This glossary lists some of the technical terms I've used in this book. You may also hear these terms when watching other videos or tutorials online. Don't let this list scare you. You do not need to know all of these. This list is for reference only. As you go through this book, if you hear a word you don't understand, look here.

Administrator / Admin - The person that is responsible for maintaining the website, adding pages, etc.

Category Silo - A silo is a closely related group of posts that link to each other but not to less related posts. For example, you might have a category on your site about mountain bikes. All posts in that category are about mountain bikes and link to other articles on mountain bikes. Categories in WordPress allow you to group posts into these silos, so you might hear the term category silo, simply meaning a group of highly related posts, all in the same category.

cPanel - This is your web host control panel that provides an easy-to-use interface and automation tools to simplify your job as site admin.

Child Theme - This is a WordPress theme that inherits its functionality from a parent theme. The parent theme needs to be installed as well as the child theme. Changes made to the child theme won't affect the parent theme, so you can update the parent theme as and when updates are available without trashing your site.

CSS - The layout and design of a web page and its contents are controlled by CSS. This stands for Cascading Style Sheets. You can change colors, font size, alignment of text or images, etc., all using CSS.

Database - A database is a file that contains information. WordPress stores your site content and settings in the database.

Dashboard - This is the WordPress control panel, where you log in to add/edit your website.

Directory (or folder) - You organize files on your computer into folders (also called directories). Web Servers are just computers, too, and files are organized into directories (or folders) on servers too.

DNS - DNS stands for Domain Name System. It's a system that converts domain names into numeric IP addresses. See also, Registrar and web host.

Domain / Domain Name - This is your website's web address. e.g., mydomain.com

FTP - Stands for File Transfer Protocol. This is a system for connecting to your webspace so you can add, edit, delete files, etc. Using a tool called an FTP client, you can view all files and folders on your server in much the same way you can with a File Explorer on your computer.

.htaccess - This is a file that is processed by your web server before your web page is loaded in a web browser. You can add specific messages to this file, e.g., to prevent certain people from accessing your site or redirecting an old URL to a new URL.

Host - See Web Host

HTTPS - HTTP defines how content is formatted and transmitted around the web as well as how web servers react to that content. HTTPS is the same as HTTP but uses SSL to ensure content is encrypted.

IP address - This is a unique string of numbers and full stops (periods) that uniquely identify a computer on the internet.

MySQL - This is an open-source database that is commonly used with WordPress installations as well as other web applications.

Plugins - Plugins are pieces of software that can plug into WordPress to add new features. e.g., a plugin might allow you to create a contact form or backup your database on a schedule.

Protocol - Essentially, a set of rules that define how something works.

Registrar - Also called the domain registrar. This is the company that registers your domain for you. They will renew it if you want to. When someone comes to your website, the registrar will send them to your web host via the DNS settings at the registrar. Each web host has a unique DNS, so the visitor will be sent to your web host, where your WordPress site is installed.

Responsive Theme - These themes adjust to the size of the web browser. If someone is viewing your site on a mobile phone, the responsive theme makes sure it looks great. The same site in a desktop browser will also look great as the responsive theme adjusts the layout accordingly.

Root folder - This is the top-level folder on your server where a website is installed. On your home computer, the root folder for any application you have installed will be the folder that contains all the files and sub-folders for that application.

RSS Feed - Stands for Rich Site Summary or Really Simple Syndication. It is a file that contains details of the last X posts on your website. Each post will have details of title, date, description, etc.

SEO - Stands for Search Engine Optimization and refers to the methods you use to try to get your site to rank higher in the search engines.

Shortcodes - A WordPress-specific code that you can use to insert something into a website. E.g., a contact form plugin may give you a shortcode like [cf-form-1]. When the page is rendered in the browser, the shortcode is replaced by the contact form.

SSL - Stands for Secure Sockets Layer. It's a security measure to ensure a connection between two computers is encrypted.

Themes - These are the "skins" of your site. They control the fonts, colors & layout of your site. You can change the look and feel of your site by changing the theme. It takes seconds to do.

URL - the web address you type into your web browser.

Web Host - This is the company that rents you disk space on their computers (servers). You can use that disk space to install your website. When someone visits your website, it's delivered from that web host. The web host has a unique DNS that you give to your registrar.

Webmaster - Same as administrator.

wp-config.php - This file contains the basic setup information for your WordPress site. Things like database name and other database settings.

Widgets - These are plug-and-play pieces of software that can add features to various areas of your website. e.g., there is a widget that displays a calendar, and this could be placed in the sidebar.

Please Leave a Review/Thought on Amazon

If you enjoyed this book, or even if you didn't, I'd love to hear your comments about it. You can leave your thoughts on the Amazon website.

www.ingramcontent.com/pod-product-compliance
Lightning Source LLC
Chambersburg PA
CBHW060150060326
40690CB00018B/4053